HOW TO CHOOSE, CHANGE, ADVANCE YOUR CAREER

HOW TO CHOOSE, CHANGE, ADVANCE YOUR CAREER

by
Adele Lewis
Bill Lewis
with
Steven Radlauer

Career Blazers Agency
New York City

BARRON'S EDUCATIONAL SERIES, INC.
Woodbury, New York • London • Toronto • Sydney

AAR C489

All inquiries should be addressed to:
Barron's Educational Series, Inc.
113 Crossways Park Drive
Woodbury, New York 11797

Library of Congress Catalog Card No. 82-13825

International Standard Book No. 0-8120-2245-9

Library of Congress Cataloging in Publication Data
Lewis, Adele Beatrice, 1927–
   How to choose—change—or advance your career.

   1. Vocational guidance.   2. Career changes.   3. Job
hunting.   I. Lewis, Bill.   II. Radlauer, Steven.
III. Title.
HF5381.L358   1982   650.1′4   82-13825
ISBN 0-8120-2245-9 (pbk.)

PRINTED IN THE UNITED STATES OF AMERICA
   3 4 5   005   9 8 7 6 5 4 3 2

CONTENTS

PART TWO   SETTING YOUR CAREER IN MOTION

PREFACE

We recently spoke with a high school guidance counselor in the Southwest who told us that he advised all his students to write long résumés, his theory being that a long résumé is more impressive than a short résumé. This was news to us, but just for the record we called a number of corporate personnel directors—the people who actually read applicants' résumés and make decisions based on those résumés—to find out what they thought about the guidance counselor's advice. Every one of them had the same response: Résumés must be short and sweet!

The point is that, while most people are exposed to general information about the employment marketplace—such as the information available from guidance counselors—hard, specific, current information, information you can trust, is available only from employment professionals who are on the inside of the marketplace.

This book is about choosing, changing, and advancing your career, all from the vantage point of professionals working in the marketplace. The purpose of Part One is to help you assess your goals and your current employment status in order to formulate your overall career strategy. In Part Two, we will help you get in touch—and stay in touch—with insiders accessible to you and with information relevant to your strategy.

Unfortunately, after over thirty years in the personnel business we have yet to discover a secret formula guaranteed to deliver anyone a dream job without his or her active participation in the process. As with anything worthwhile, you will have to make an effort for the plan to succeed. We are convinced, though, that our advice and your effort are a winning combination, and that, in a surprisingly short time, you'll be ready to enter the marketplace with strength, confidence, and a clear sense of direction.

PART ONE

YOU AND YOUR JOB

MAKING DECISIONS

Some Basic Premises about Work

It should come as no surprise to learn that you spend more time in bed than anyplace else. Seven or eight hours a night, every night of your life—that's a lot of sleep! What's the next most popular place? A few simple calculations reveal that most of us spend the lion's share of our waking hours at work. Look at the figures:

$$\frac{5 \text{ working days}}{\text{a week}} \times \frac{50 \text{ working weeks}}{\text{a year}} \times \frac{42 \text{ years (an average}}{\text{working lifetime)}} =$$

10,500 7-hour days

or

73,500 hours

or

28.77 years

Any way you count, it's a lot of time. Now, no sane person would deliberately spend twenty-eight years sleeping on an uncomfortable bed; yet how many people spend their entire working lives stuck in an unpleasant job? It's a sad fact of our society that many who have no trouble making decisions about where to have dinner, which TV show to watch, what brand of toothpaste to use, or where to go on vacation simply *don't* make intelligent decisions about something infinitely more important: their careers.

Whether you like it or not, work is an inescapable, integral component of your life, not an activity conducted in a vacuum. An unhappy day at the office usually makes for an unhappy evening at home; an unhappy *career* can certainly contribute to an unhappy *life*.

It's obvious that work helps shape the meaning of our lives—for better or worse. The question is, What's keeping *you* from a career in which you can express your beliefs and goals, exercise your creativity, and experience satisfaction?

We've found that what's holding many people back is that, somewhere along the line, they assimilated the myth that *work* is synonymous with *pain*. This belief is a real showstopper; if you believe it, what's the point of going on? It is, however, an easy myth to dispel—there are in this world countless examples of individuals who actually derive enjoyment from their work. This brings us to the first premise of our book:

It Is Important to Feel Good About Your Work

The desire to find a career that feels right is the engine that will power your job search.

Another popular myth that stops people in their tracks is that all jobs are tedious drudgework. Belief in this ridiculous myth gives it the status of a self-fulfilling prophecy. Since there are no good jobs, I won't bother looking for a good job, and I'll settle for whatever comes along. You, however, know better; and if you don't, you're about to. The second premise of our book:

Good Jobs and Good Careers Exist!

They can be found, developed, invented, obtained, and fallen into. In other words, there's no need for *you* to be stuck doing something you hate for the next 73,500 hours. We're going to help you figure out exactly what constitutes a good career for you, then help you devise a strategy whereby you'll get the job that sets your career in motion.

This happens to be a very interesting time in which to be expanding one's career horizons. There is a greater variety of career opportunities available now than at any previous time, and new career paths are opening up at a breathtaking rate. Of course, in this state of rapid flux, some traditional careers may be on the way out; however, the sophisticated job seeker can easily avoid training for a position that no longer exists or applying for work with a company that's about to go belly-up. We'll show you how to keep right on top of the situation.

Yes, good jobs do exist, but what about secure jobs? In the old days, a clerk, for example, might have been perfectly content to keep his job for the entire forty- or fifty-year span of his career. Today, however, the situation is a bit more unstable. Divisions are taken over by other divisions. Companies move to other regions or are taken over by other companies. A clerk might be fired for no better reason than that his supervisor—who originally hired him—is being fired.

The fact is that, today, the clerk who sticks around to receive a gold watch after twenty-five years of loyal service is no longer looked upon as the ideal employee. In many industries, in fact, frequent job-hopping—as long as the job-hopper is moving up rather than down or sideways—is regarded as a sign of success. And in some industries, the only way to get anywhere is to skip from one company to another as frequently as possible. Our third premise:

True Security Resides in You, Not in Your Job

Real security is in your ability to do a job—and to *find* a job. Expertise in finding and changing jobs is not an innate ability, nor is it something taught in schools. It is a skill which, for most, is so infrequently required that it is never perfected. In fact, it is rarely even regarded as a skill in its own right. We'd bet that if you spoke with a number of people who have recently changed jobs, you'd find that the vast majority spent more time planning their last vacations than organizing the strategies for their career moves.

THE HIDDEN JOB SKILL

In order to get a job, an applicant has to possess all the qualifications required by the employer, right? Well, yes and no. For some jobs, of course, certain qualifications are essential. The partners of a law firm, for example, would never consider taking on a new lawyer who hadn't completed law school and passed the bar exam. However, in many cases, the employer sets out a list of qualifications designed primarily to limit the number of applicants and to weed out those who might be less serious about the job. In reality, it is not unusual to find that the person who gets the job does not precisely meet all the qualifications; and there are many who have landed excellent positions for which, on paper, they were eminently unqualified. These people possess the hidden job skill, the skill that no employer will ever ask you about and that no want ad will ever mention. This skill—*the ability to plan a strategic career move and get the job you want*—is perhaps the most important single job skill you will ever possess.

In a sense, learning to plan career strategy is like learning to fly an airplane. One of the first things a student pilot is taught is to be constantly on the lookout for a place to land in an emergency. It becomes a habit of every good pilot to glance at the ground several times a minute, looking for a flat field or a deserted stretch of highway on which he may land the plane safely. Likewise, a career-conscious person is always keeping an eye out for potential career opportunities as well as for any potential career crises that might arise. This alertness should become second nature.

Once you have mastered this important skill, you'll never again have to feel insecure about your career. You'll know that when the time comes, you'll be able to spot an opportunity when it presents itself and end up right where you want to be.

Successful Job Hunting and Finding

The following are some key elements in the job search and how this book will help you become familiar with them—our job-hunting strategy.

Know Yourself; Know What You Want

A surprising number of the applicants we have met over the years have been utterly without a clue as to what they're looking for. Some have never stopped to think about who they are, what they'd like to do, and what their needs are. Some know what they like but don't see how it will help them plan a career. Many, upon learning what the job marketplace is really like, are ready to throw in the towel because they don't see how their needs are compatible with those of industry.

We feel that the first step in a successful job hunt is to start knowing yourself better. We'll present a systematic approach to self-knowledge, at least insofar as it pertains to your career strategy. Our goal here will be to make sure you're as realistic as possible in assessing your skills, your desires, your education and training, your work history, and your personality.

Know the Job Marketplace

What's going on "out there" is a big mystery to many job seekers. Those who are entering the marketplace usually carry with them mythical pictures of how their careers are going to go. Invariably, they are surprised when they see firsthand how things really work. Those who want to change careers are often confused about the internal operations of industries different from the ones in which they are currently employed. And returnees to the work force very often are out of touch with the current employment situation.

While we haven't the space in one book to detail the internal operations of every industry, we do have some handy ways to find out exactly what you need to know about those that interest you. In addition to directing you to pertinent information sources, we'll show you how to enlist the aid of employment experts; how to get assistance from family, friends, and acquaintances who are in positions to help you; and how to gain firsthand experience in an industry without making a long-term commitment to a specific job.

Make Your Decisions . . . and Act on Them

All right, you've analyzed yourself, you've studied the job marketplace, and you're still not sure what your next step ought to be. What now?

We'll help you *decide to decide*. We'll show you how, once you've made a decision, you'll have a whole new vantage point from which to view the world—with particular emphasis on that corner of the world in which you intend to conduct your career. We'll help you see how, in the early stages of a career, it's almost impossible to make a "wrong" decision, as any thoughtful decision will take you in the right direction by advancing your knowledge of yourself, the industry, and the job marketplace. We'll show you how to capitalize on every step so that it brings you a greater store of information, expertise and confidence, and puts you in a better position for your next career move.

Find a Good Job

Of course! From packaging yourself and preparing your résumé, locating appropriate job openings, and approaching the right person in the right organization, to negotiating your salary at the conclusion of a satisfactory interview—we'll guide you through the entire process. We'll even give you pointers on how to keep your career growing after you've started your new job.

Career Blazing—
Beyond the Job

Finding a job is, of course, important; but even more important than finding a job is *building a career for yourself*. Often, finding a good job is synonymous with making a good career move, but sometimes the right career move might be to take a job that's not so good *now* but will grow into something a little further down the line. How will you know which job is good for your career and which isn't? We'll help you learn.

Keep Informed

The more highly informed you are, the more likely you are to make the right decisions. Almost any situation will present you with a constantly changing matrix of information. Hirings and firings, the overall performance of the economy, a personal preference of a corporate superior, a job opening with a competitor—any number of disparate elements can affect the course of your career. It is important to remember that you are not operating in a vacuum. Start now, even before your job search begins in earnest, to keep your eyes and ears open for information that may be of value to you.

Be Flexible

In addition to being open to new information, it is important that you be flexible in its applications. It's one thing to hear about a new industry trend; it's quite another to be ready to go with that trend. It's career suicide to think of yourself as knowing all you need to know— be prepared to learn new skills, to change tracks, to *grow* with the flow.

Move When Advantageous·

Staying at a job that has grown stale, unpleasant, or just plain boring is not only a drain on your energy but it's also bad for your career.

We'll help you recognize whether the problem lies with the job itself, with your career path, or with you; then we'll help you figure out what to do about it. The key is to be prepared to take action, especially if that action involves switching jobs or even switching careers.

One last note on decisions: you are always making decisions, whether you know it or not. Even *not* deciding is a decision—*the decision not to decide*. As long as you can't avoid it, you might as well start out with the attitude that you're not going to run from decisions but that you're ready to decide to decide. With that decision behind you, you're ready to launch your career strategy.

2

ASSESSING YOUR JOB AND YOUR CAREER

Do You Like Your Job?

We assume that you have at least some reservations about your present job; if you didn't, you probably wouldn't be reading this book. What we'd like to do now is to help you think analytically about your job and your *feelings* about your job. The key here will be to separate the momentary ups and downs from the long-term perspective. Anyone can have a bad day, or a good day for that matter; what's important is the overall effect.

One of the key factors affecting the way you perceive your job is its career potential. If you know the job is going nowhere, you're likely to be upset by everything from major personality clashes to minor annoyances. Conversely, with a job that has career advancement potential, you will probably find yourself ignoring many of the problems that would otherwise annoy you.

Regina, a young woman who had been a journalism major in college, was working as an administrative assistant with an import-export firm. She'd been there almost a year but already had grown restless. Everything in the office was beginning to get on her nerves, from the constantly ringing phones to the color of the walls. By the time she came to see us, she was a nervous wreck. We helped her find another administrative assistant's job, this time with a monthly magazine. When she came in for a visit a couple of months later, she was a very different young woman; she had calmed down and was quite happy with her job. What was ironic was that her new job was essentially the same as her last one—answering phones, filing, and typing. The difference was that the new job held advancement potential, which put the day-to-day annoyances into proper perspective. Interestingly, Regina was getting paid slightly *less* at the new job than at the old one—publishers are not famous for their largess—yet she insisted that she was much happier than she had been before.

Obviously, the trick is to be able to see your job *in context*. A job which fits in with your overall career plans—even if the job itself is not that great—will make you happier than one which doesn't relate to your desired career.

For those who are unhappy with their present job but who aren't quite sure why, we have prepared an informal questionnaire to help determine the degree of dissatisfaction.

Sunday Night Questionnaire

A sampling of job applicants was asked to complete the sentence "On Sunday night, I feel . . ." The ten words or phrases that follow are representative of their responses, and we use these to help you determine how you feel about work. Score each phrase on a scale of 1 to 5, depending on how closely it reflects your feelings; 1 means you never feel that way, 5 means you usually feel that way. Circle the appropriate number, then total up the numbers circled.

"On Sunday night, I feel . . . "

1. like playing hooky tomorrow. 1 2 3 4 5

2.	exhausted.	1 2 3 4 5
3.	like my brain is atrophying.	1 2 3 4 5
4.	boxed in.	1 2 3 4 5
5.	frustrated.	1 2 3 4 5
6.	like I'm wasting my time.	1 2 3 4 5
7.	like I'm going to quit soon.	1 2 3 4 5
8.	fine about tomorrow . . . but what about next week or next year?	1 2 3 4 5
9.	like hitting my boss.	1 2 3 4 5
10.	like a square peg in a round hole.	1 2 3 4 5

TOTAL _____

If you scored 15 or under, consider yourself lucky; you are happy with your job. If you scored 15 to 30, you are in a borderline situation; your job's positive and negative attributes are roughly in balance.

If you scored between 30 and 40, you're ready to move on to a new job. And if you scored over 40, now just calm down! Don't quit until you've planned your strategy.

Obviously, this is not a scientific experiment but rather a tuning-up exercise. In Chapter 3, we'll take a much closer look at your job-related problems with an eye toward determining the exact cause of these problems.

Evaluate Your Present Job

Let's move on to our Job Evaluation Form (page 14), the purpose of which is to help you focus objectively on your current job. Take the time now to go through the questionnaire and check off the items that pertain to you.

JOB EVALUATION FORM
(check or fill-in the appropriate boxes)

1. THE EMPLOYER:

   (A) Size: ☐ Small—under 50 employees
   ☐ Medium—between 50 and 150 employees
   ☐ Large—over 150 employees

   (B) The installation in which you work is:
   ☐ Headquarters for the organization
   ☐ An important branch office
   ☐ A smaller branch office

   (C) Type of organization:
   ☐ Manufacturer
   ☐ Provider of a service or services
   ☐ Retail business
   ☐ Wholesale distributor
   ☐ Nonprofit organization

2. YOUR POSITION:

   (A) Title or position:_____

   (B) Your position within the corporate structure:

   Who is above you?_____

   _____

   _____

   Who is below you?_____

   _____

   _____

   (C) Your responsibilities:_____

   _____

   _____

3. TANGIBLE REWARDS OF YOUR JOB:

☐ Good salary
☐ Good benefits
☐ Expense account
☐ Travel
☐ Responsibility
☐ Seniority
☐ Other:_____

_____

4. INTANGIBLE REWARDS OF YOUR JOB:

☐ Prestige
☐ Security
☐ Fulfillment
☐ Glamour
☐ Recognition/Identity
☐ Other:_____

_____

5. NEGATIVE ASPECTS OF YOUR JOB:

☐ Tension
☐ Salary and benefits not good enough
☐ Unfulfilling
☐ Boring
☐ Not what you want to do
☐ Too much travel
☐ Not enough responsibility
☐ Too much responsibility
☐ Other:_____

_____

6. ENVIRONMENT:

(A) Physical environment:
☐ Office
☐ Factory
☐ School/Laboratory
☐ Farm/Field
☐ Other:_____

(B) Location:
- ☐ Work at home
- ☐ Short commute
- ☐ Long commute

(C) Social interaction:
- ☐ Work alone
- ☐ Light contact with others
- ☐ Moderate contact with others
- ☐ Constant contact with others

7. CAREER POTENTIAL

- ☐ Little or none
- ☐ Advancement possible within organization
- ☐ Advancement possible by moving to another organization
- ☐ Higher salary/advancement possible within position
- ☐ More responsibility possible within position
- ☐ Greater power and influence possible within organization
- ☐ Other:_____

Categories 3, 4, 5, and 7 are the most objective parts of this form. Almost everyone will agree on the meaning of these points; that is, a good salary is a benefit, excessive on-the-job tension is not a benefit, and so forth.

The other categories have no objective values independent of *your* value system. For example, your goal may be to work in a big city, while someone else might want to be a dairy farmer. If you are currently working on a farm, your check next to "Farm/Field" under "Environment" is definitely not a plus; for the other person, however, this environment is perfect.

Going back to Categories 1, 2, and 6, pick out the items you have checked that you regard as *negative* and underline them. Do not underline those entries which are neutral or positive.

As an example, let's assume that Joe Califano is currently a production supervisor for a manufacturer. He spends part of his day in an office and part in a factory. His daily commute from home takes an hour and fifteen minutes each way. In the office part of his job, he deals with other supervisors, upper management, and customers. In the factory, he deals with hordes of quality control people, line supervisors, and assembly line workers. Category 6 of his hypothetical Job Evaluation Form might look as follows—*after* he finishes underlining the negative points.

6. ENVIRONMENT:

    (A) Physical environment:
        ☒ Office
        ☒ <u>Factory</u>
        ☐ School/Laboratory
        ☐ Farm/Field
        ☐ Other: _____

    (B) Location:
        ☐ Work at home
        ☐ Short commute
        ☒ Long commute

    (C) Social interaction:
        ☐ Work alone
        ☐ Light contact with others
        ☒ Moderate contact with others
        ☒ <u>Constant contact with others</u>

So, according to this hypothetical form, Joe doesn't mind working in the office but dislikes the factory part of his job; the commute doesn't bother him; and the heavy contact (in the factory side of his work) is unpleasant. Although undeveloped, a pattern is beginning to emerge.

Let's now go back to your form. Does it resemble the hypothetical example, with some entries underlined and others not underlined? Or did you underline everything? or nothing? Don't worry if you see no trace of a pattern emerging yet—there'll be plenty of time for that later. What is important now is to try to observe your job objectively, as though you were an outsider to your own life. We'll draw conclusions later.

Career
Considerations
Points to Ponder

It's relatively easy to describe your feelings about your job; after all, you're face to face with it every day. Considering your *career,* on the other hand, may be more difficult. A job has a concrete reality, while a career may seem a good deal more abstract, less tangible.

Before moving on to the next chapter, which will explore the exact nature of any problems you may have with your current job, take a minute and complete the simple yes/no questionnaire below. It is designed to start you thinking about the answer to the question "Is my current job in line with my career goals?"

Once you've completed the questionnaire move on to Chapter 3 to discover exactly what is wrong with your current job.

FROM JOB TO CAREER

YES	NO	
( )	( )	My current job is satisfying.
( )	( )	I enjoy working in this field.
( )	( )	I can imagine working in this field for at least three more years.
( )	( )	I can imagine working in this field for at least five more years.
( )	( )	I can imagine working in this field indefinitely.
( )	( )	There are no limits on my ability to grow in this field.
( )	( )	My job leads logically and directly to the career of my choice.
( )	( )	I don't need more education or experience in order to advance my career.
( )	( )	There is no immediate need to switch companies or organizations in order to advance my career.

3

WHAT'S WRONG WITH YOUR CURRENT SITUATION?

Although it may seem that all your problems are caused by your job, there are actually three closely related areas from which most employment problems stem: problems caused by your *job*, problems caused by your *career*, and problems caused by *you*.

Problems with Your Job

It is easy to blame our problems on our jobs. There are even segments of our society where it is considered normal to hate our jobs. However, it is dangerous to blame the job for the problems unless there is a really good reason to do so.

A genuine job problem is one that is rooted in the specific position you hold with your current employer. For example,

- Your boss habitually promotes his dim-witted nephews instead of you.

- Your company has been sold to a conglomerate that is famous for firing all the employees of the companies it acquires.

- Your supervisor is having marital difficulties and likes to take out his problems on you.

- You've been advising the vice-president that it's time to install a computer. The vice-president insists that computers are a passing fad.

- You have to crawl through a swamp to get to your office every morning.

Although experiences like these can make going to work a bitter experience, it is important to contain your animosity and recognize the problem for what it is. It is not uncommon for people to misinterpret a problem that is rooted in a specific job and extrapolate that problem to encompass an entire field. Obviously, this is unfair to the particular field; it may also cause a kink in your career plans.

A good example of this is Cathy Riley's experience, related in her own words.

I'm a vice-president of one of New York's oldest investment banking firms, and I'll tell you this—I didn't get here the easy way. Not that it's been such a struggle; I *have* worked hard, but there's one terrible decision I especially regret.

I started out after college with a bank that, at the time, had a reputation for taking interesting risks, usually favorable ones. Unfortunately, they weren't much interested in taking any risks on a woman, and so after they'd passed me over for a promotion in favor of a man who had far less on the ball than I had, I found myself a job at another bank right across the street.

I was doing very well at my second job. In fact, I think that, at the time, I was probably moving up the corporate ladder faster than anyone else with the company. Then it happened; I got my third promotion within twenty-four months—and I almost died. It was my boss, a senior vice-president. He must have hated me or hated all women or something. Whatever it was, he made my life miserable. Nothing I did was right. He'd spring traps on me just to show everyone how stupid I was. It was horrible.

I stuck it out for another year, and finally I couldn't stand it anymore. I couldn't sleep, I wasn't eating right, my husband kept telling me that I ought to start seeing a psychologist about my "problem." Well, I knew what my problem was, or at least I thought I knew. I handed in my letter of resignation and swore I'd never again take a job in banking.

Well, let's see. I worked with my husband in real estate for a while, I worked selling insurance, I even went back to school for a couple of years to get my MBA. And then, about ten years after I'd quit my banking job, you know what? I decided to give banking another try.

I was hired as an administrative assistant, and the rest is history. Within four years, vice-president.

Do you know why? First of all, I must say, immodestly, that I'm very good at what I do. Second of all, and I guess this has something to do with the first point, I *love* banking; I just love it. I always did. Even though I went through ten years of telling everyone how much I despised the business, I secretly knew that I was, well, born to be a banker. What I didn't realize was that it wasn't banking I despised; it was that miserable senior vice-president who insisted on torturing me.

If only I knew then what I know now, I could have quit, waltzed into another firm, and who knows—I'd probably be chairperson of the board by now!

Because Ms. Riley misinterpreted her problem, she lost ten valuable years, during which time she could have been enjoying herself in her chosen field and building her career. The irony is that because it is easier to change jobs within a given profession than it is to break into that profession, Ms. Riley would have had an easier time getting an executive position with another bank (while she was still employed in the job she disliked) than she eventually had in getting the administrative assistant position ten years later.

The moral is, Be Wary. If you are dissatisfied with your work and are considering hopping to a new field, take a close look at the following specifics before you do anything drastic.

1. Personalities: Do your co-workers or supervisors make it impossible for you to do a good job?

2. Duties or Responsibilities: Do your assignments include many items that are inane, repetitive, impossible to accomplish, or outside your field of expertise?

3. Promotional considerations: Are you consistently passed over or ignored at promotion time, while less qualified individuals are moving ahead of you?

4. Mergers and acquisitions: Is your job about to be adversely affected by outside forces?

5. Poor management: Do you feel that those in charge are consistently making the wrong decisions?

6. Physical arrangements: Do you have an overly long commute? Are you working in an under-heated office? These conditions can leave you feeling bad about your job.

7. Are there other specifics that apply only to *this particular job* but not necessarily to the field or industry as a whole?

Examine your problems closely. You may find that it is not the job or the work, per se, that bothers you but the specific difficulties that go along with your particular organization. If this is the case, you probably would be perfectly happy staying on your career course but changing organizations to one that was free of these problems.

Problems with Your Career

What if you have the nicest boss in the world, a great salary, a company car, a fabulous office all to yourself, good fringe benefits, and you *still* dread going to work in the morning? It sounds like you could have the right job—but in the wrong field.

A career problem is rooted not in your specific, current position but in the field in which you are employed. For example,

- You have recently hopped from one company to another one in the same field—at a considerably higher salary and with a better title. After four months, you realize that you're still unhappy with your work.

- You've just received a raise and a new office, and the president of the company indicates that you are in line for vice-president. Instead of making you happy, this news gives you a feeling of claustrophobia.

- You're good at working with figures, but working in an office gives you the creeps. All you want to do is work outdoors as a farmhand, a ranchhand, or a school crossing guard. Why, you wonder, do you always end up in some airless room doing bookkeeping?

- Your parents insisted that you go to law school or medical school or dog-training school. Now you find yourself in a job that doesn't make any sense.

Diagnosing a career problem can be tricky. It is perfectly conceivable that you are not cut out to be a lawyer. This does not mean that you think it is a *bad* profession, only that it is not the right one for you. However, many people experience a certain type of pressure—from their peers, their parents, or themselves—which makes them feel guilty and foolish for turning their backs on an entire profession. It's what we call the Sixty-Million-Lawyers-Can't-Be-Wrong syndrome. Although you know that a given field is not for you, you end up succumbing to the pressure of numbers. Obviously, this is no way to make an important career decision.

Career problems are sometimes interpreted as job problems. People who have been working in a field for a number of years can find themselves settling into that field even though it's doing them more harm than good. By imagining that their problem is a specific job problem, they never have to venture outside the safety of their known world when looking for another position. Thomas Canzone's story is a good illustration of how this can happen.

I've recently left, at the age of thirty-eight, a successful career in the advertising business. I started out doing layout when I was fresh out of college. Pretty soon they had me doing illustrations in addition to layout, and then I stopped doing layout altogether and stuck to illustration. It didn't take long until I was in charge of a group of five or six artists and making big bucks. And I was bored stiff.

I figured it was because of the people I worked with—the dullest bunch on Madison Avenue. So I mentioned my predicament to a few friends at other agencies, and before I knew it, job offers started coming at me. In the back of my mind, I guess, I knew I would never really be happy in advertising, but I was flattered to be getting job offers, and I rationalized that, surely, I would be having a better time at some other agency.

I took the most interesting job that came my way, a job with a small shop that had just gotten a multimillion dollar contract with a major cosmetics manufacturer to do all their TV commercials. And they wanted me to be the head designer for the entire operation.

I must say, I learned a hell of a lot on that job. But after a few years, I found my mind wandering again. And again I rationalized the problem. I told myself that my company had grown too fast, that everyone had grown too conscious of the bottom line, and that no one was paying attention to the quality of the work anymore. I started looking around for something else, something, perhaps, in publishing, but before I could get too serious, another job offer came my way. It seemed like an offer I couldn't refuse.

This one was with another TV commercial production house, one that specialized in high quality commercials for one or two huge clients. It sounded great, and I leapt at it. But I realized right away that it wasn't for me. Not that there was anything wrong with the job or the company or the clients—they were all top-notch. What I realized was that I simply had had it with advertising, and no amount of money, no new jobs, nothing could change that. I also realized that if I didn't do something soon, I might be stuck in advertising for the rest of my life, and I got scared.

So I quit the new job after only a few months. My advertising buddies thought I'd flipped my wig, but I knew exactly what I was doing. I took a deep breath and hit the street—for the first time since I had left college. I went out looking for freelance illustration jobs, something where I could work where I wanted and when I wanted, with the freedom to pick and choose those jobs that appealed to me. It took awhile, but I finally hooked up with two magazines which liked my work and gave me a choice of assignments, assignments I liked. So far, it's worked out great. I work three or four days a week on the magazine assignments, and the rest of the time, I work on my own painting.

It's what I should have been doing in the first place, probably. It just took me a long time—after I started in my illustrious advertising career—to build up the courage to venture out of that world. I guess I didn't like the idea of being anonymous after building up a reputation in advertising. Anyway, I'm glad I finally got up my nerve.

Mr. Canzone's story is a classic example of someone changing jobs when what was really needed was a change of *careers*. Although it would have been to Ms. Riley's advantage to find another job in banking while still employed as assistant to the senior vice-president, it would have been to Mr. Canzone's advantage to get out of advertising entirely as soon as he realized it was not for him, regardless of how easy it was for him to find another position in this field.

The moral of this story is, once again, Be Wary. If you are dissatisfied with your work, take a close look first at your particular position, and if upon examination that doesn't yield an answer, look at the field itself. Consider the following to see if your problems might be *career* problems.

1. You don't enjoy the work, regardless of how well you do it or how quickly you are advancing in the field.

2. You feel like you're not going anywhere, even though, by objective standards, you're making fine progress.

3. You have a history of changing jobs within the field; yet you don't feel that there is any progression, just succession.

4. You have a habit of finding petty faults with your job, your organization, your supervisors, your co-workers—despite the fact that it's really a pretty good job.

5. You feel guilty that you don't feel better about your work.

When you work in a given field, you develop relationships, you gain a reputation, you feel comfortable. In most fields, a camaraderie develops, even among competitors. It is like living in a small town or being a member of a large extended family; it is difficult to leave when the time comes. Many people fool themselves into thinking that there is something wrong with their specific jobs when, in fact, the problem is that they're working in the wrong field. Their fear of the unknown overpowers their common sense, and they end up with a succession of new jobs in the same field, new jobs that have no real advantages over the old ones.

What they don't realize is that they'll never find the right job in the wrong field.

Problems with You

Are you working as a paralegal and resentful that you haven't received a promotion in six months, although there's no real opportunity for promotion because you haven't been to law school? Do you feel boxed-in teaching English although, as an English major, you can't think of anything else you're qualified to do? Does it anger you that, as an administrative assistant, you're expected to produce perfect letters all day long although you feel you're overqualified for the job? Are you beginning to feel that all employment agencies are phonies because none of them can find you a $25,000-a-year entry-level job with a nonprofit organization? We hate to say it, but it sounds like the problem lies within yourself.

The personal problems most commonly encountered are categorized below.

Attitude Problems

There are several common varieties of attitude problems prevalent nowadays. People with bad work habits constitute the first group. These are the ones who refuse to understand the importance—for their own sake—of doing a good job wherever they work. The secretary who is lazy about proofreading, the administrative assistant who loses important notes, the law clerk who is continually late to work—they are all doing their careers a great disservice. They have in common the desire to move ahead, to get a job that utilizes their talents. They also have in common an ignorance about how careers are built—progressively, with one job leading to the next, each one better than the one that went before. They'll never move on to the next job if they're making a mess of their current jobs. They don't see that their current jobs represent a passport to something better. Employers check references; sloppy work habits will be reported, making it very difficult for the sloppy worker to move ahead. People with bad work habits often think that they are cheating their employers with their insouciant attitude, but they are wrong; they are cheating only themselves.

Another common attitude problem is what we call the Prima Donna syndrome. People with this problem resist admitting to themselves that, regardless of how creative, artistic, and special they may be, they still need to find a job in order to pay the rent. When they are finally forced by circumstances into taking a job, they are too proud to make a wholehearted effort. To their employers, they don't look like creative, talented people—just lazy employees.

These are the very people who, once they get with the program, often go on to have stellar careers in their chosen fields. Their problem is that they hate to admit they're just starting out, thereby ignoring the very positions that are open to them. Once they realize that they'd better start making an effort, they find that there are plenty of opportunities for them to exercise their creativity.

To these people, we emphasize the importance of making that effort, of really committing oneself, even if the situation seems less than perfect. Get started first; you'll have plenty of time to attain your goals once your career starts to take shape.

A third type of attitude problem is what we call the "Blinders" syndrome. These are the ones who, for one reason or other, think that the grass is greener every place else. If they are currently employed, they are certain that their company is the worst one in its field or that their job is the worst one in the company. If they are looking for work, they act insulted when told that they'll have to know how to type in order to get a certain job. We know them from our viewpoint as the job seekers who tend to go out on interview after interview, finding every possible reason why this company is bad and why that company doesn't understand how things work.

We have come to the conclusion that their blinders are really a defense mechanism cleverly designed to postpone any decision making. Strangely enough, the blinders mysteriously come off when it's time to get down to business; these people are perfectly capable of doing excellent work when they finally deign to get serious about their careers. Our advice to this group is blunt: We're not going to be able to help you until you're willing to help yourselves. Come back when you're ready to get serious.

If you think you have an attitude problem, remember this—you are the only one who can do anything about it. A bad attitude can undermine the best-laid career plans. And what can be more foolish than undermining your own plans?

Unrealistic Job Seekers

These are people who are looking for work as nuclear physicists in Monaco or entry-level jobs with nonprofit organizations that pay $25,000 a year. If they are employed, their unrealistic expectations may lead to unwarranted aversion to their present jobs. (They may be *deliberately* avoiding the truth; incidentally, see the above section on the blinders syndrome.) If they are straight out of school, they may feel confused and disappointed because the working world isn't the way they expected it to be. There are no jobs for nuclear scientists in Monaco or $25,000 entry-level jobs with nonprofit organizations.

Generally, we can straighten out these folks by simply introducing them to the facts. Most are ready to accept the facts and start looking for a job that actually exists or accept their current position to be not so bad when measured against reality. Those few who resist the facts most certainly fit into the attitude problem category.

Personal Problems

Everyone has problems. No one is expected to fully separate his personal life from his professional one. Every employer knows that there are personal crises that must take precedence over work—from time to time.

There are, however, people who are habituated to living in a crisis state. They're the ones who are always getting phone calls in the middle of the work day from their wives, husbands, girl friends, boy-friends, friend-friends, baby-sitters, house-sitters, dog-walkers, law-yers, accountants, and bail bondsmen—all with bad news. Invariably, the bad news breaks their concentration and that of their co-workers. These people, regardless of how good their work is, quickly get a reputation for being troublemakers, which can severely hamper career advancement.

Persistent personal problems that interfere with your ability to do your job, irrespective of their origin, must be regarded as *your* re-sponsibility. If you feel that your problems are holding you back, don't complain about them; *do* something about them. If you feel, "I'd be doing well except for ———," it's time you took responsi-bility for whatever the problem is, solve it, and get down to business. If you feel that the problem with your job is that your co-workers lack compassion, perhaps it's time to examine what you are doing to bring out their lack of compassion. After all, they're not your psychologists, and they probably have their own personal problems to deal with.

Lack of Education, Training, or Experience

Has it been a little too long since your last promotion? Does it seem that people who arrived after you did are moving ahead at a faster rate? Do you find yourself expecting a promotion, only to find that a new person from outside has been hired to fill a vacancy you thought was yours? Have you been trying to find a job for weeks or months with no success? Perhaps your lack of education, training, or expe-rience is the cause.

In Chapter 6, we'll detail the educational opportunities available today; for now, suffice it to say that there has never been a time like the present for accessible, inexpensive educational opportunities. Any-one who feels that he or she has missed the boat educationally is missing the point—further training is available to anyone who wants it.

Furthermore, most employers nowadays realize that continuing education is good for both organization and employee. Employees who inform their employers of their decision to upgrade themselves often find that they are looked upon with new respect, and it is not uncommon for raises or promotions to come even before the training is completed. Job seekers who include their adult-education history in their résumés have an edge over those whose thirst for knowledge seems to have ended once they left school.

And, of course, there are those careers which are simply impossible to enter without the right educational background. It used to be impossible for a late bloomer to enter a profession such as medicine or law, but today there are more and more people making those decisions well into their 30s, 40s, and beyond.

So, don't be afraid to come to the conclusion that your education is holding you back. If it is, now's the time to face the problem squarely, decide that it's time for a change, and *take action*.

A Note to the Returnee

The returnee to the work force faces a number of unique reentry problems such as a lack of confidence in skills that haven't been used for years, unfamiliarity with the current state of the job marketplace, fear of being subject to age prejudice, or lack of a résumé with continuous work experience.

There were grounds for these problems and fears in the past but, fortunately, those days are gone forever. The fact is that today many employers actively seek to recruit returnees. Returnees—mostly women who have taken a number of years off to raise a family—are regarded in the current employment marketplace as ideal applicants. While many young applicants are viewed as being flighty, undisciplined, and unbusinesslike, returnees are considered steady, hardworking, and professional. It is reasoned that anyone who was able to raise a family and maintain a household is a seasoned veteran, perfectly capable of carrying out any assignment.

All across the land, skills-training centers are springing up to remedy the problems that many returnees face. Quick brush-up courses in typing, for example, in the space of two or three weeks, can bring back the returnee's long-lost confidence in her typing skill. (An entire division of Career Blazers is devoted to just this type of advanced, effective, and inexpensive skill training.) Many returnees have actually jumped right into the burgeoning electronic office fields, using such skills as word processing, with greater ease than their younger co-workers.

As for the other problems—unfamiliarity with the job marketplace, age prejudice, lack of a résumé with continuous work experience—these really aren't problems at all. Most returnees probably understand the marketplace better than young high school and college graduates who are just entering it; the returnee has already been through it. And although some of the names have changed, the game remains the same. Any good employment agency counselor can fill in the details and answer specific questions about the local employment scene. As for age prejudice, as we've said, that may have been a problem at one time, but, for the most part, that is a thing of the past. (Furthermore, there are now laws against age discrimination.) Résumés? Most returnees *have* continuous work experience; if raising a family isn't work, then what is? (More on résumés in Chapter 8.)

Where Do Your Problems Lie?

Let's go back to your Sunday Night Questionnaire, your Job Evaluation Form, and your "From Job to Career" questionnaire with an eye to diagnosing exactly where your problems lie. Look over these three forms. If there are any changes you'd like to make, make them now. Then, keeping in mind all you have read so far, complete the three-part questionnaire below in the same way you completed the Sunday Night Questionnaire—on a scale of 1 to 5, with 1 representing those areas in which you never experience problems and 5 representing those areas in which you often have problems. If you've answered the questions honestly, the results will indicate whether your major problems lie with your specific job, your current field, with you, or with any combination of the above.

ANALYSIS OF CURRENT SITUATION

I. *PROBLEMS WITH YOUR JOB:* In my current job, my problems are:

		SCORE
1.	Personalities clash	1 2 3 4 5
2.	My assignments are unsatisfying	1 2 3 4 5
3.	I'm not getting promoted	1 2 3 4 5
4.	Outside forces (such as a merger) are about to adversely affect my situation	1 2 3 4 5
5.	The company is poorly managed	1 2 3 4 5
6.	The physical arrangements are bad	1 2 3 4 5
7.	Other:_____	1 2 3 4 5

TOTAL, PART I:

II. *PROBLEMS WITH YOUR CAREER:* In my career, I find:

1.	I don't enjoy work	1 2 3 4 5
2.	It never feels like I'm progressing	1 2 3 4 5
3.	I change jobs but never feel like I'm going anywhere	1 2 3 4 5
4.	No matter how good the job is, I find fault with it	1 2 3 4 5
5.	I feel guilty that I don't feel better about my work	1 2 3 4 5
6.	The entire field is on the downswing	1 2 3 4 5
7.	Other:_____	1 2 3 4 5

TOTAL, PART II:

III. *PROBLEMS WITH YOU:* I think that the following problems can be traced to me:

SCORE

1.	I have bad work habits	1 2 3 4 5
2.	I'm a prima donna	1 2 3 4 5
3.	I think my situation is bad because I don't know what's going on elsewhere	1 2 3 4 5
4.	I'm unrealistic/uninformed	1 2 3 4 5
5.	I let personal problems interfere with my work	1 2 3 4 5
6.	I lack the education, training, or experience I need to advance in my career	1 2 3 4 5
7.	Other:_____	1 2 3 4 5

TOTAL, PART III:

The totals are

PART I (job):_____ PART II (career):_____ PART III (you):_____

Now comes the hard part—what to do about it. It's easy enough to *say* you should change jobs, switch careers, jettison your attitudes and habits, or get the education you need; but actually making the tough decisions can be another matter altogether. Rather than leaping immediately into action, let's take a look at what you need from a job and how important it is to know how what you need fits in with the realities of the job marketplace.

4

THE PERFECT JOB

We recently asked a sampling of job applicants the question "What do you want from your job?" The responses were as varied as the job applicants themselves.

"I want to do something that's *fun*."

"I'd like a chance to learn from an expert, a real mentor who can show me how to do it right."

"I want to work with people."

"I don't care what I do, as long as I get to travel a lot."

"All I care about is my family. As long as I can support them and spend a lot of time with them, I'm doing fine."

"I want to work with my hands."

"I want a nice easy job so when I come home at night, I'm not all tired out."

"I'm looking for a job as a production assistant because I want to be a television producer someday."

"I need a temporary job to keep a roof over my head until my next acting part comes along."

Although we usually assume that *income* means "money," in reality we each have a slightly different concept of what kind of income we're looking for. The young actress, between parts, can't afford to take a full-time position because she would have no time to take classes or try out for parts. The middle-aged woman who is returning to the work force after a twenty-year absence may be looking for something that will help her to ease back into the working world; getting a top salary is not her primary consideration. The young man or woman with an MBA may be looking for a first job that pays a top salary without regard to where the company is located or what business it is in.

Knowing
What Is Important
for You

The various types of incomes may be divided into two major categories, "material" income and "psychological" income. Here are several examples of each.

PSYCHOLOGICAL INCOME

glamour
security
prestige
fulfillment
identity
social
potential (leading to future benefits)

MATERIAL INCOME

money
benefits (medical, insurance, dental, etc.)
expense account
company car

Material income is immediate, tangible, and easy to define. Psychological income tends to be less immediate, intangible, and more difficult to define. In most instances, the line between the two is easy to see; in other cases, the line becomes hazy. For example, the young actress with the temporary job has a need for what may be termed "pragmatic" income—a job that pays the rent between acting assignments but will not interfere once she gets an acting job. Pragmatic income fits nicely into both material and psychological income categories. In any event, the distinction is useful in helping us to determine what our real needs are.

Most of us have a variety of income needs. We need money, we like to feel satisfied with our work, we enjoy spending time with our families and friends, etc. We do not, however, all have the *same* income needs. Charting your own income profile is an essential step in the formulation of your career strategy. It will only take a few minutes, but if you've never thought this through before, it can save you a good deal of time later on.

The first step is to take another look at the incomes chart. Can you think of any other types of psychological or material incomes? If so, write them down here.

PSYCHOLOGICAL _____

_____

MATERIAL _____

_____

Now, referring to both our list and yours, list in order of priority the five types of income that are most important to you, regardless of which category they fall into.

1. _____

2. _____

3. _____

4. _____

5. _____

It's all right if you can't think of five. Our MBA's list looked something like this:

1. _____ *money* _____

2. _____ *money* _____

3. _____ *money* _____

4. _____ *expense account* _____

5. _____ *money* _____

Our returning housewife, on the other hand, had a list that looked like this:

1. _____ *social (work with people)* _____

2. _____ *fulfillment* _____

3. _____ *money* _____

4. _____ *security* _____

5. _____

Is your number-one income priority in the number-one position on your list? If not, change it now, to avoid having to think things through all over again later. Once you have settled on your number-one income priority, write it down below.

My number-one income priority is _____.

Why separate the number-one priority from the others? First, to underline your top choice—to plant the seed now so that in Chapter 6, when it's time to recall these choices, you will have had plenty of time to think it over. Second, to have it readily available in case it becomes necessary to choose between a job that has everything *but* your top income priority and one that has your top income priority but little else. Setting priorities in advance helps avoid making aberrant choices later.

Aberrant Choices—
What Not To Do

Let's take a look at some examples of what may happen if you do not spend a little time examining your own current situation, your hopes and desires, and the state of the job marketplace in your community.

There is always the chance that you'll get lucky and, without doing any preliminary work, end up in just the right place at the right time and fall into the perfect job. What is more likely is that you will find a job that gives you nothing more than a paycheck and that you give nothing more than seven or eight hours a day. How long can you keep a job that isn't right for you? Six months? A year? Three years? Many people do it—but why you? Take the time to analyze your situation now and you can skip right over the Wrong Job syndrome.

People are endlessly inventive when it comes to finding themselves jobs they can't stand, but their techniques usually can be reduced to one of these three categories of miscalculation.

1. Underestimating themselves
2. Overestimating themselves
3. Avoiding the issue and listening to someone else's estimation.

The following stories from our files illustrate the problems encountered by an underestimator, an overestimator, and an avoider.

The Underestimator

Jack O'Connor seemed too young to be retiring, but that is exactly what he was about to do. Over a thirty-year career in the fire department, Jack had worked his way up through the ranks to captain. Now, at the age of fifty-one, he was coming to Career Blazers to see if we could find him some part-time work to supplement his pension and give him something to do.

When our counselor asked him what type of work he was looking for, Jack was not very optimistic. He felt that although he was an excellent fire fighter, he was not qualified to do anything else. He was thinking of becoming a part-time clerk or salesman. However, when the alert counselor began to question him as to what exactly his responsibilities were with the fire department, the picture that emerged was much more impressive than the one Captain O'Connor was painting of himself.

He had thirty or more men working under him. He knew all about buildings—he'd been fighting fires in them and inspecting them for a long time. He knew as much as anyone could know about construction materials and how they were used, and he knew all the suppliers and most of the contractors in the area. There was a lot of paperwork that went along with the job but, Jack explained, he usually had no trouble getting a couple of the younger lieutenants to do that sort of thing.

"Jack," the counselor asked, "how much do you think you should be earning?"

"Oh, I don't know," he said. "My pension's not bad. I guess I could get by with seven or eight thousand dollars a year. That's not bad for part-time, is it?"

"Well, I suppose, if that's what you want. But look, you've got some very unusual qualifications. You know this city better than any-one—you know the construction business, you know landlords, you have lots of experience designating responsibility, you have a good head for administration."

"Gosh, when you say it that way, it really sounds like something."

"Jack, it sounds like you're an executive. In the construction industry. And a good one at that. And for a lot more than eight thousand a year. I bet we could have you starting for twenty-five, maybe even thirty thousand dollars a year with your experience. What do you think?"

He thought about it for a minute, then he smiled. "I guess you could talk me into it."

It took a few weeks, but we did find Jack O'Connor a job—as vice-president of purchasing for a small but rapidly expanding construction company. Although he was surprised that anyone would hire *him* for such an important position, it took him only a couple of weeks to get right into the swing of things. The last we heard, the firm was growing faster than ever, Jack had hired a few people to work under him, and he was contemplating a European vacation for the first time in his life. A part-time clerk indeed!

The Overestimator

The hustle and bustle of the office stopped dead for a moment when she stepped through the door; she was dazzling. Her hair was long, blond, and expensively coiffed. Her nails were perfect. Her shoes were expensive. She looked like she was on her way to the opera or to a gallery opening, and she was just popping her head in to see if there happened to be any jobs waiting for her at Career Blazers.

Her name was Carole Byorkman. She had recently graduated from one of the more prestigious universities on the East Coast, having majored in English with a minor in journalism. She'd spent her junior year at Oxford. She had a thirty-page résumé complete with 8 × 10 glossy photos, letters of recommendation from professors on two continents, and her complete college transcript. She asked if we thought we could find her a job in the editorial department of a national magazine; we assured her we would do our best.

There was no problem in lining up interviews for her—her credentials were excellent, she presented herself well, she seemed a perfect candidate for an entry-level job in magazine publishing. After her fourth interview, however, her counselor realized that something was wrong; Carole's smile was gone, and her friendly look had been replaced by a rather nasty scowl.

"I'm not going to be a *secretary*," she said to her counselor when he asked her what was wrong. "I told you I wanted to write a column, and you keep sending me to jobs where I'm supposed to sit by the phone and type all day. And the worst insult is the pay they expect me to take. I don't see what's so hard about telling them I'm not a secretary; I'm a *journalist*. Maybe I ought to try some other agency."

"Carole," the counselor patiently explained, "no one, *no one* gets hired to be a journalist right out of college, at least not on a major national magazine. You've got to understand that we're sending you to very good *entry-level* jobs in the field. If you do well, you can start moving up the ladder in a year or so—sometimes even sooner if a little luck is involved."

"And what about the pay?" Carole interrupted. "I've never heard of such low-paying jobs."

"Well," said the counselor, "we could try to find you something in another field."

"I don't want something in another field; I want to write for a magazine!"

"All right, then, you'll have to get something straight. Entry-level publishing jobs are not high-paying jobs. Ever. They don't have to be. It's one of the 'glamour' industries, where there are dozens of applicants for every job opening. Understand? Why, there is at least one major publisher which pays less than a living wage just to keep the number of applicants down to a minimum. And you know what? People are *fighting* for those jobs!"

"Really?"

"Yes, really. Now I suggest you get your priorities straight. Either you want a job in publishing or you don't. If you do, the only kind of job you're qualified for—I don't care what your résumé says!—is an entry-level job at entry-level pay." He took a deep breath, then continued. "I think, Carole, that you'd be very good in that field. But if you really want to do it, you'll have to realize that there are a limited number of job openings and lots of competition for every one of them. If you're not interested, I'm sure we can find you something in another field—for a lot more money, too."

"No, wait," Carole said. "I didn't realize how it worked. Maybe . . . maybe I should go back to the last magazine. I think they really wanted me, and it looked like a pretty good situation, even if I did have to answer the phone and type a lot."

Carole was smart enough to take her counselor's words to heart. She was offered the job, and she took it. Although it was not quite the journalism job she had dreamed about, it took her only a couple of weeks to realize how lucky she was to have landed it at all—many qualified people were *still* applying for the job long after she had been hired. The big surprise was how different magazine work was from the way she had imagined it. With every day, she learned something new, and with everything she learned, she realized how much more there was to know. Her original attitude, she now knew, had little to do with the real world; the entry-level job was exactly what she needed to teach her what it was all about and to give her an inside line on any promotions that might come along.

How do we know all this? About ten months after she started with the magazine, Carole was tapped to take over the position of a junior editor who had unexpectedly moved on to another magazine. She was calling to tell her counselor of her good luck, to thank him for not allowing her to go off enraged ten months earlier, and to say that Career Blazers would probably be getting a call from the magazine's director of personnel to order a new administrative assistant—for Carole!

The Avoider

Scott Lehman came to Career Blazers directly after graduating from law school. This itself was unusual; law school graduates often have jobs lined up through connections they made in school. What was even more unusual about Scott was that he was coming from a very highly respected law school where he'd graduated third in his class.

Placing him was easy; a fine Manhattan law firm interviewed Scott and made him a lucrative offer his first day out. He accepted and went right to work under the wing of one of the firm's senior partners whose specialty was entertainment law. His career seemed to be well on its way.

It came as a big surprise when, some eight months later, we noticed Scott's name in the morning paper in connection with a show business scandal. An actress's lawyer, it seems, had made off with some of her personal papers, selling them to a national gossip magazine. The actress was in the process of suing the lawyer, and it appeared that he might go to jail if found guilty. The bar association had already suspended him. The lawyer's name was Scott Lehman.

We didn't see how it could be the same bright young lawyer we'd placed—why would he do something so foolish? It was there in all the papers, in black and white, and yet we just couldn't believe it. That's when he waltzed into our office for the second time.

Scott admitted cheerfully that he was, indeed, the lawyer involved in the scandal; he almost seemed proud of it. Then he asked if we thought we could find him another job. The strangest part was that he wasn't looking for work as an attorney; he wanted an entry-level job in *advertising*. Scott's original counselor, realizing that something strange was afoot, sat down with him to hear his story.

Scott, it seemed, had grown up in a family of lawyers. His father, his grandfathers, and uncles and aunts on both sides of his family were lawyers. From as far back as he could remember, everyone had assumed that he would be a lawyer when he grew up.

He went along with his family through high school, through college, and right through law school. Although he'd never really fancied the idea of being a lawyer, he didn't know what else he wanted to do and so he went with the flow. Then, in his final year of law school, he became fascinated with the advertising industry. Feeling, however, that it was too late to change his life's plan, he ignored his fascination and continued working hard, getting good grades—and hating every minute of it.

In his job with the law firm, Scott had to keep reminding himself of how lucky he was, how well he was doing, what a terrific career he had in front of him. By his third month, he was severely depressed, feeling that he was doomed to spend the rest of his life "imprisoned" in a career that wasn't his. In the midst of his depression, he hit upon a way to get out.

It was, he admitted, childish, immature, foolish—but effective. By getting caught stealing his client's letters, he was ensuring that he'd never again find work as an attorney, at least not with one of the better law firms. It was only by taking such a drastic step, he said, that he could guarantee that his parents would not be able to convince him to go back to being an attorney.

"I only wish I'd been able to ignore my family or override their wishes earlier," Scott said sadly. "It would have saved all this pain and embarrassment, and it sure would have saved me a lot of time. And you know what the ironic part is? As soon as my parents and the rest of the family overcame their shock about the whole thing, they became incredibly supportive. They asked me why I didn't tell them ten years ago that I didn't want to be a lawyer. Can you beat that?"

Scott's story is an extreme example of what may result from avoiding a thorough evaluation of yourself, the objective conditions of the job marketplace, and the way they might fit comfortably together. By heeding other people's opinions, however well-meaning, he allowed himself to be railroaded into a corner from which a graceful escape was all but impossible. Looking back on it, he considers himself lucky to have escaped when he did. Fortunately, the actress finally decided to withdraw her lawsuit; we found Scott a job with an advertising agency, and though he's not making as much money now as when he was an attorney, he's happy for the first time in many years.

Are you ready to decide to take control of your career? Then don't fall into the traps of being an overestimator, an underestimator, or an avoider. By systematically examining your needs, your likes and dislikes, your skills and educational background, you'll have an excellent shot at matching what you have to offer with what the world "out there" is looking for.

In the following chapters, we'll show you how to determine exactly what it is that the local job marketplace is seeking—not only in general terms but in the specific, day-to-day terms of your local community. We'll even help you figure out how to get paid while you gain experience and learn the ins and outs of the local job scene. Stay tuned.

HOW DO YOU RATE AS AN EMPLOYEE?

Every employee, from the shipping clerk to the president of any organization, is constantly being judged as to how well he or she is performing on the job. The judgment may be as casual as an occasional pat on the back—or cryptic reprimand—or as elaborate as a formalized monthly rating system. Whatever the system and whether it is implied or overt, your "ratings" play an important role in both your day-to-day functioning and your overall career program. Having good ratings, aside from making your work day a little more pleasant, can increase the frequency of raises and promotions; bad ratings can have a discouragingly dampening effect on your career plans. Having a good understanding of what employers look for in their employees can help you in a number of ways.

- It will increase your objectivity. Seeing yourself through the eyes of an imaginary employer reveals qualities in yourself, both positive and negative, that you probably never knew you possessed.

- It will help as a diagnostic tool. Seeing yourself from an employer's point of view will show you which of your weak points you need to work on and which of your strong points should be nurtured.

- It will serve as an aid to résumé writing and interviewing. You don't have to worry about either of these for a while, but it is a great help to start thinking like an employer now so that it will be second nature by the time you're ready to write your résumé and take your interviews.

- Obviously, understanding what employers look for in employees can be of great benefit once you are employed in a new position. Remember, the purpose of being a good employee is not to see how many brownie points you can score with your employer but rather to hasten the progress of your career. Assuming you have done your homework and have obtained the right position, what's good for your employer is good for your career.

Over the course of your career, you'll probably have dealings with a number of different employers or supervisors, and each will rate your work with a different set of criteria. We have found, however, that most employers are looking for essentially the same qualities; the differences from one organization to the next are usually quite minor and often can only be discovered after you have been hired.

The Other Side of the Coin

The Employee Evaluation Form on page 49 is an example of the type of rating system used by many organizations, both large and small. It will help you to see specifically what employers, even those who do not have such a formal system, consider important in their employees. Following the blank form, we'll show you some examples of how employers fill in such forms.

EMPLOYEE EVALUATION FORM

EMPLOYEE:_____

TITLE:_____

DATE EMPLOYED:_____

IN PRESENT POSITION

SINCE:_____

DATE OF

THIS APPRAISAL:_____

DATE OF

LAST APPRAISAL:_____

RATED BY:_____

TITLE OF RATER:_____

INSTRUCTIONS: This form is to be prepared by a director or department head. Ratings *must* be supported by narrative comments and discussed with the employee, especially in regard to suggested corrections for employee's weaknesses and suggested means of encouraging employee's strengths.

	POOR	FAIR	GOOD	VERY GOOD	EXC.
1. JOB EXPERIENCE/KNOWL-EDGE	( )	( )	( )	( )	( )

Does employee have sufficient job experience, knowledge, and training to handle present assignment?

_____
_____
_____

	POOR	FAIR	GOOD	VERY GOOD	EXC.
2. UTILIZATION OF RE-SOURCES	( )	( )	( )	( )	( )

Is employee effective in utilizing equipment, time, money, materials, space, staff services, and manpower?

_____
_____
_____

3. QUALITY OF WORK   ( )   ( )   ( )   ( )   ( )

Does employee maintain
satisfactory standards of
quality in completion of all
assigned tasks?

4. QUANTITY OF WORK   ( )   ( )   ( )   ( )   ( )

Does employee maintain
satisfactory production
standards and report status
of output?

5. DEPENDABILITY   ( )   ( )   ( )   ( )   ( )

Can employee be trusted to
complete all job assign-
ments in a satisfactory
manner?

6. WILLINGNESS TO ACCEPT
    RESPONSIBILITY   ( )   ( )   ( )   ( )   ( )

Is employee cooperative in
accepting existing, addi-
tional, and new job responsibilities?

7. JUDGMENT   ( )   ( )   ( )   ( )   ( )

Does employee maintain an
awareness of all responsibilities and act in the best interest of the company?

8. ATTENDANCE/PUNCTUAL-
    ITY   ( )   ( )   ( )   ( )   ( )

Is employee punctual and is
attendance good?

9. EMOTIONAL RESOURCES
   AND TEMPERAMENT   ( )   ( )   ( )   ( )   ( )

Does employee withstand
job pressures without losing
control and assist in maintaining a calm, constructive
atmosphere?

10. ORGANIZATION   ( )   ( )   ( )   ( )   ( )

Does employee maintain an
orderly work area for the effective planning, coordina-
tion, control, and completion of all assigned tasks?

11. DEVELOPMENT OF OTH-
    ERS   ( )   ( )   ( )   ( )   ( )

Is employee effective in re-
cognizing, developing, and
utilizing the potential of fellow employees and/or sub-
ordinates?

12. LEADERSHIP ABILITY   ( )   ( )   ( )   ( )   ( )

Is employee effective in obtaining support of others to
accomplish objectives, follow procedures, and accept
his/her suggestions?

13. INSPIRATIONAL ABILITY   ( )   ( )   ( )   ( )   ( )

Does employee inspire others with confidence, re-
spect, and desire to do a
better job?

14. ADAPTABILITY   ( )   ( )   ( )   ( )   ( )

Does employee adapt well
to new policies and procedures?

15. ORIGINALITY/INITIATIVE   ( ) ( ) ( ) ( ) ( )

Is employee willing to make
decisions and institute new
methods and procedures?

_____

_____

_____

16. MENTAL ATTITUDE   ( ) ( ) ( ) ( ) ( )

Does employee cheerfully
contribute to company goals
and attempt to assure the
safety, comfort, and positive attitude of all employees?

_____

_____

_____

17. SUITABILITY   ( ) ( ) ( ) ( ) ( )

Is employee suited to his/
her present position?

_____

_____

_____

18. RELATIONSHIPS
   A) Respected by superiors   ( ) ( ) ( ) ( ) ( )

   B) Respected by peers   ( ) ( ) ( ) ( ) ( )

   C) Respected by subordi-
      nates   ( ) ( ) ( ) ( ) ( )

   D) Respected by outside
      contacts   ( ) ( ) ( ) ( ) ( )

19. PROMOTABILITY   ( ) ( ) ( ) ( ) ( )

Does employee exhibit the
required skill, knowledge,
and desire to perform be-
yond present capacity?

_____

_____

_____

( ) Capable of advancing to_____

( ) Presently at capacity

( ) Has already exceeded capacity

( ) Not in position long enough to rate

20. OVERALL RECOMMENDATIONS AND EVALUATIONS

_____

_____

_____

_____

_____

_____

_____

21. SALARY

Salary change recommended: ( ) YES   ( ) NO

Proposed increase $_____

Proposed annual salary $_____

Requested by:

Dept. Head/Manager_____

Approved by:

Director_____

Personnel Director_____

Treasurer/Controller_____

Date requested:_____

Date effective:_____

22. EMPLOYEE COMMENTS

_____

_____

_____

_____

_____

_____   _____
Employee's signature   Date

    This questionnaire was adapted from forms submitted to us by a variety of organizations in several different fields. A number of the forms had already been filled in by supervisory personnel; a sample of both positive and negative responses is shown below.

POSITIVE RESPONSES

	POOR	FAIR	GOOD	VERY GOOD	EXC.

2. UTILIZATION OF RESOURCES

Is employee effective in utilizing equipment, time, money, materials, space, staff services, and manpower?

( ) ( ) ( ) (X) ( )

Knows her department inside-out.

3. QUALITY OF WORK

Does employee maintain satisfactory standards of quality in completion of all assigned tasks?

( ) ( ) ( ) (X) ( )

Work rarely contains errors - is clean and well put together

6. WILLINGNESS TO ACCEPT RESPONSIBILITY

Is employee cooperative in accepting existing, additional, and new job responsibilities?

( ) ( ) ( ) ( ) (X)

Always.

12. LEADERSHIP ABILITY

Is employee effective in obtaining support of others to accomplish objectives, follow procedures, and accept his/her suggestions?

( ) ( ) (X) ( ) ( )

Does it hisself rather than designates—good listener—respected by all.

NEGATIVE RESPONSES

	POOR	FAIR	GOOD	VERY GOOD	EXC.

2. UTILIZATION OF RESOURCES

Is employee effective in utilizing equipment, time, money, materials, space, staff services, and manpower?

(X) ( ) ( ) ( ) ( )

She always seems to find the most complicated way of doing a job.

3. QUALITY OF WORK

Does employee maintain satisfactory standards of quality in completion of all assigned tasks?

( ) (X) ( ) ( ) ( )

Many errors—wastes time doing same work over and over again.

6. WILLINGNESS TO ACCEPT RESPONSIBILITY

Is employee cooperative in accepting existing, additional, and new job responsibilities?

( ) (X) ( ) ( ) ( )

Tends to pass responsibility on to others.

12. LEADERSHIP ABILITY

Is employee effective in obtaining support of others to accomplish objectives, follow procedures, and accept his/her suggestions?

(X) ( ) ( ) ( ) ( )

Has no credibility with other employees. Terrible !!

As you can see by the negative responses, employers don't pull punches in their evaluation of employees. At the same time, the positive responses show that employers and supervisors do take notice of a job well done.

Did you notice that there were no outlandish or arcane categories on the Employee Evaluation Form? This is because employers do not waste their time seeking out and hiring people with unusual, extraordinary, or glamorous qualities unless, of course, the job requires those qualities for a specific reason. What most employers cherish are the basic, fundamental qualities that make possible the day-to-day operation of any organization.

How would you rate yourself on an Employee Evaluation Form? Imagine for a moment that you are your own employer. Go back to the blank Employee Evaluation Form and fill it in with *your* rating based on your performance in your current job, or how you would expect yourself to perform in your next job. Be tough on yourself!

The Fundamentals

Did you notice that there were no mysterious questions on the Employee Evaluation Form? Nothing about the employee's blood sugar level, ability to perform complex negotiations, or moviegoing habits—just plain, old-fashioned common sense questions about the employee's ability to perform in the day-to-day environment.

Such innocuous "tasks" as coming to work on time every day, looking reasonably neat, being friendly and courteous to fellow employees and clients, and keeping your work space relatively clean can make a big impression on your supervisor/employer. Of course, none of this makes any difference if you are not getting your work done. However, assuming that you are doing a reasonably good job with your work, paying attention to these fundamentals practically guarantees you a place in the organizational "fast lane" when it comes time for raises and promotions.

Why make so much fuss about things which should be common sense to everyone? The fact is, sadly, that a sizeable proportion of today's work force has lost touch with the fundamentals of working.

When we get a complaint about someone we have placed with a corporate client, nine out of ten times, it is not a complaint about the applicant's typing speed or ability to handle angry customers or any other *functional* problem. It is about the applicant's way of dressing or habit of coming in fifteen minutes late every morning or taking an extra long lunch break every day. In other words, complaints about that person's ignorance of the fundamentals of work.

There will never be a time in your career when you'll be able to discard these fundamentals. Usually, in fact, those at the top are even more scrupulous than those nearer the bottom of any hierarchy in their regard for the fundamentals. How many times, for example, have you heard it said that the president of such and such a corporation is a workaholic? How many times have you heard it said that the filing clerk is a workaholic?

Professional athletes—perhaps more clearly than the rest of us— understand the importance of the fundamentals. A baseball player, for example, even one who earns a half-million dollars a year, spends some time before every game warming up, shagging flies, taking batting practice, fielding grounders, and running wind sprints. The only difference between the professional ballplayer's warm-ups and those of the eight-year-old Little Leaguer is that the professional spends an hour or two warming up while the Little Leaguer spends only fifteen minutes. The professional and his manager realize that whatever he does is built on top of his foundation of fundamentals and that he's never too good to ignore the fundamentals while pursuing the more exotic aspects of the sport.

The fundamentals of career building are within your grasp: there are no fundamental secrets that you don't already know. *Common sense* is the key, and common sense is not something that only a PhD can grasp. It is really just a matter of being well-groomed, courteous, easy to get along with, and hardworking. If you are able to keep a level head in any situation, all the better. As simple as it seems, you'll find that by attending to the common sense fundamentals, you'll be much happier, no matter what you are doing. And when it's employee evaluation time and your supervisor starts weighing the pluses and minuses, we're sure that you'll be right up there with the best of them—like cream rising to the top.

Your Assets and Liabilities

When you've completed your own Employee Evaluation, translate your rating into a simple chart. Using the blank chart below, check either the "asset" or the "liability" box.

EMPLOYEE ASSETS AND LIABILITIES

CATEGORY	ASSET	LIABILITY
1. Job experience/knowledge		
2. Utilization of resources		
3. Quality of work		
4. Quantity of work		
5. Dependability		
6. Responsibility		
7. Judgment		
8. Attendance/ punctuality		
9. Emotional resources/temperament		
10. Organization		
11. Development of others		
12. Leadership ability		
13. Inspirational ability		
14. Adaptability		
15. Originality/initiative		
16. Mental attitude		
17. *Suitability		
18. *Relationships: superiors		
19. *Relationships: peers		

20. *Relationships: subordinates

21. *Relationships: outside contacts

22. *Promotability:

*Categories 17 through 22, marked with an asterisk (*), may be left blank if you are not currently employed.

In Chapter 3, we discussed problems with your specific job, problems with your career, and problems with you. You'll notice that almost all the Employee Evaluation Form categories, if evaluated as liabilities, are problems with *you*. The reason behind this is clear; from your employer's point of view, the specific job—and the entire field, for that matter—is a given. That is, your employer is not about to change his or her organization to accommodate your particular tastes. *You* are the only variable in the equation. You are judged by the standards of the organization on your ability to function within the organization's parameters.

You would have to be a perfect employee—or a highly prejudiced judge of your own capabilities—to have survived this rating without earning at least one or two liability points. Many people actually tend to *under*rate themselves when presented with this type of questionnaire. There are two reasons for this.

1. People about to enter the job market tend to be unsure of themselves and undervalue their abilities.

2. Many job seekers imagine that employers are only interested in finding people with extraordinary abilities, educations, and backgrounds.

In fact, as we have said before, employers are primarily concerned with finding people with common sense and a good command of the fundamentals. You are as capable as anyone else of getting to the office on time, being responsible, and dressing neatly. Chances are good that your liabilities are, for the most part, simple attitude problems that you should have no problem overcoming. Let's take a look at those liabilities.

Liabilities

Except for categories such as "job experience/knowledge," most of your liabilities reflect attitudes that you hold about yourself. To remedy a lack of experience or knowledge, you will most likely have to go outside yourself by getting a job which will give you the information you lack or by enrolling in the appropriate training institution. To remedy an attitude problem, however, you need go no further than yourself. Except in cases that involve a severe psychological problem, such as an acute problem in dealing with authority figures, most attitude problems are no more than the lingering bad habits picked up in childhood, school, and previous work experience. Bad habits, though tenacious, are made to be broken; if they are hampering the progress of your career, you have all the reason in the world to break them.

Divide your liabilities into those that are attitude problems and those that are genuine lacks or gaps in your education, work history, or background; then list them.

ATTITUDE PROBLEMS

1. _____

2. _____

3. _____

4. _____

5. _____

LACKS, GAPS

1. _____

2. _____

3. _____

4. _____

5. _____

Depending on your ultimate career choices, not every liability will prove detrimental to the progress of your career. For example, such categories as "development of others" and "leadership ability" may not be important to someone whose career goal is to write advertising copy or be an opera singer. Many of the categories, however, will prove liabilities regardless of your career choice. "Quality of work," "dependability," "responsibility," "judgment," "attendance/punctuality," "emotional resources/temperament," "organization," and "mental attitude" are all important *assets* to a serious job hunter regardless of career choice.

If you have listed liabilities that can be detrimental to your career, circle them now. Take a look at any attitude problems you have circled. Is there any reason why you cannot solve these problems yourself as part of your career strategy? On a large piece of paper, write down your reasons for *not* solving these problems.

And here is our reason why you *must* start working on the solutions to these attitude problems: *Your career and your happiness depend on it.* Now write down how you will start to solve these problems. Be prepared to refer back to this when you feel your resolve slipping!

Have you circled any liabilities in the "lacks, gaps" column? If you know how to solve these problems, write down the solutions.

The next chapter contains information on educational opportunities, skill training, and other ways to gain valuable experience to give your career a boost.

Many people regard their liabilities as innate parts of their personalities. How many times have you heard someone say, "I'm lazy" or "I'm sloppy" or "It's impossible for me to wake up on time"? Well, that may be fine for them, but it's not good enough for *you*. You are the one who wants to land a good job and move your career into the fast lane, right? Overcoming your liabilities, particularly the attitude problems, is an important component of your career strategy and a great personal challenge. You've come too far to let yourself down now.

Assets

We told you to be tough on yourself, which means that the assets you've listed are above suspicion. It is always helpful, however, to have some evidence with which to back up your claims, especially when those claims are being presented to a potential employer. Your assets and the evidence behind them will come in very handy when you are putting together your résumé. Take the time now to jot down some notes to back up the assets that you have listed. For example, let's say that "adaptability" is one of your assets. Let's further assume that you consider yourself adaptable because you've moved within your company from department to department and location to location and always managed to learn the territory in a matter of a week or two. Your notes might read, "Able to function in various departments and locations."

	ASSET	EVIDENCE
1.	_____	_____
2.	_____	_____
3.	_____	_____
4.	_____	_____
5.	_____	_____
6.	_____	_____

Matching Your Assets with Your Priorities

The relationship between your assets and your income priorities (from Chapter 4) is an important factor in determining your career direction. If the relationship is a stormy one, you may find your career movement grinding to a halt. For example, if your top priority is to work in a highly social environment, but your team abilities, such as leadership, inspirational ability, and develoment of others, are nonexistent, you've got problems.

But, as with the other career problems, a solution is at hand. Chances are that one side, priorities or assets, is more highly developed than the other. Let's assume that your top priority is something near and dear to your heart, something you have been dreaming about and working toward all your life. No lack of abilities is going to stop you from getting what you want. Even if you have to take classes in group behavior or find a job in which you are forced to deal with lots of people, you'll find a way to develop the skills you need to land the job you want. If, on the other hand, your priorities are wishy-washy, but your assets are crystal clear, you'll probably feel no regrets about ignoring your priorities and following your assets wherever they may lead. Let's assume that you'd like to work in a social environment, but it's not an overpowering need. Your skills, education, and previous work experience are all in a field in which you spent a good deal of time working alone. Furthermore, you are good at what you do, you are on an interesting career track, and you enjoy your work. Our advice would be to stick with your assets and continue to develop your career. We predict that the time is not far off when you'll have accumulated enough power, or savvy, to change your career path in such a way that you'll be using your skills *and* dealing with people without any conflict of interests.

If it will help you see more clearly, list your priorities side by side with your assets. Do your assets and your priorities complement each other? Are they in conflict with each other? Which are stronger or more important to you, your assets or your priorities? Would it make sense at this time to reevaluate your priorities? To start working on augmenting your assets?

The importance of getting your assets and your priorities in tune with each other cannot be overstated. A little further down the line, when it's time to present yourself in the job marketplace, you'll have a much better time of it if you're able to show a unified front to your contacts, personnel agents, and prospective employers. With your assets arrayed, your priorities aligned, and your self-ratings high, you'll have no trouble convincing any of them that you're the one they're looking for.

6

A NEW CAREER?

The field you are working in should challenge your abilities and spark your imagination. A job which doesn't engage your strengths or which is more demanding of your weak points than your strong points is not likely to keep you interested for long or be a logical launching pad for your career.

This chapter is for you if:

- You are unhappy with your present career direction and are ready for a change
- You have had a series of jobs that led nowhere
- You are returning to work after a long absence and don't know where to begin.

Narrowing Your Choice

If you have read this far, you know the importance of being realistic in your career plans. Thinking realistically, you should eliminate any thoughts of embarking on a job search for:

1. A job requiring extensive training or advanced degrees that you cannot realistically acquire

2. A job requiring experience that you don't have

3. A job requiring physical traits, talents, or expertise that you don't have and can't acquire quickly.

This is not to say that jobs with such requirements are completely out of the question for you. However, if you plan to make your move *soon,* you should choose a path that will give you the experience, skills, or training you need—or the time and money to acquire them.

A career is the course of one's work over a period of time. An intelligent approach to career planning requires that you have faith in time itself—in the fact that there is a future and that the decisions you make now will have repercussions in that future. Your decisions *now* are seeds that will come to maturity *later.* Because you are the one who will be harvesting the fruits, it behooves you to be aware of what you are planting.

To continue the metaphor, you simply don't have time to plant every possible seed at this moment. You may have perfect freedom to pursue any number of career directions, but that is only because you have yet to start making career decisions. These decisions, in a sense, limit your freedom. The decision to go to medical school, for example, makes it impossible to go to law school at the same time; the decision to be a lumberjack in Oregon makes it impossible to be a tennis pro in Miami at the same time.

Narrowing down your career choices is a process by which you decide, for the time being at least, *not* to do some of the things you may previously have considered doing. People who are afraid of making decisions are usually afraid of missing out on something; by taking the left fork of a road, they don't get to see what's up the right fork, and vice versa. Therefore, they decide not to decide and spend the rest of their days standing in the middle of the fork watching the traffic go by. Fortunately, no career decision is irrevocable; changing careers is possible at any age, with no stigma attached. What's important is to consider all the possibilities, rule out the ones that are less appealing to you, and take a good long look at the remainder. And, as we've

WELCOME TO THE '80S

Starting in the late '60s and continuing through the '70s, a deluge of a certain type of career advice book hit the market. These books had in common a '60s "do your own thing" attitude, an upbeat, super-optimistic feel, a flippant style, and a game playing approach to finding a job. They claimed that all you had to do to find your dream job was to list the things you like to do best, make a few phone calls, and a job would materialize with your name on it. These books were very popular. There were days when nearly every Career Blazers applicant would enter our offices with one of these books in hand.

What may have made sense in the '60s and '70s is beginning to look awfully dated here in the '80s; there have been a lot of changes in the past decade, and not all of them bode well for the employment situation. You've probably noticed that we have not emphasized how easy it is to land the ideal job with the ideal salary in the ideal location. What we have been emphasizing is that if you do your homework, if you analyze your likes and dislikes to see how they can best mesh with the real-world marketplace, and if, finally, you are willing to *work* at your current job or your new job, you'll be well on the way to being in control of your career.

Starting with this chapter, we will show you how to start making your career decisions and how to act on those decisions, how to speed up your job search, how to present yourself to best advantage and to whom, how to keep your career moving after you've started a new job, and lots of other information that is useful in the *current* marketplace. No tricks, no games, no blue-sky schemes. The good jobs and good careers are still there for the getting, but it's a tight market and you're liable to find yourself up against some formidable competition. Anyone who tells you otherwise is a dreamer or an outright charlatan. We're here to help you formulate your goals and to make it easier for you to meet them—perhaps to even show you a shortcut or two. What we can't do is to do *your* work for you; what we won't do is to pretend that things are easier than they really are. The purpose of this book is to help you choose, change, or advance your career—not to give you a sense of euphoria while you wait for your dream job to materialize.

said before, if you can't seem to find any job or career that really appeals to you, the best thing to do is to choose anyway, even if it's a "lesser of several evils" choice. After you have made the decision and take action by going out and getting a job in the field, you'll find that everything changes; you'll have a much better vantage point from which to judge that field and other related fields as well. Once you're on the inside, it won't take you long to clarify your sense of direction and fine-tune your career goals.

In the remaining pages of this chapter, you will have the opportunity to rank those careers that are of interest to you according to a rating system you have already devised—the income ratings from Chapter 4. The purpose of these ratings is to give you a chance to see all the fields you've ever considered lined up side by side so that you can consider how they compare with each other in providing you with what you need from a career. The purpose is *not* to make you reject all careers except the top one; if things were that simple, you probably wouldn't need to be going through all this in the first place.

Table 1 is a list of those careers which, according to the U.S. Department of Labor, will require the greatest number of new recruits over the next decade. This information will be particularly useful to those who have not as yet made any career choice and are looking for a good bet or who are looking for a career that is not likely to suffer from future economic downturns or who simply enjoy the idea of being in demand.

In addition, Table 2 lists occupations cited by the Department of Labor as predicted to show job-opening increases of over 50 percent of current figures by 1990.

If you find yourself at a loss for knowing job or career titles and if the above lists don't help, you may need to do some research. Probably the fastest and most convenient way to find out about the employment situation in your community is to buy the local paper and study the help-wanted section. If that doesn't give you any ideas, it is worth a trip to your library to have a look at the classic book on the subject, the U.S. Bureau of Labor Statistics' huge *Occupational Outlook Handbook*. If your library does not have a copy, you may obtain one

Table 1.
U.S. DEPARTMENT OF LABOR'S TOP 25 GROWTH OCCUPATIONS
(THROUGH THE EARLY '90s)

OCCUPATION	ESTIMATED NUMBER OF NEW JOBS
Secretaries, stenographers	875,000
Local truck drivers	400,000
Cooks, chefs	266,250
Registered nurses	240,000
Machinists	171,900
Welders	165,000
Teachers' aides	160,000
Carpenters	151,500
Construction-machinery operators	150,000
Engineering and science technicians	146,250
Retail sales workers	135,000
Accountants	129,750
Police officers	125,000
Real estate agents/brokers	112,500
Construction workers	107,250
Automobile mechanics	105,000
Lawyers	99,000
Bookkeepers	85,000
Computer operators	84,750
Labor-relations workers	83,750
Social workers	82,500
Beauticians	82,100
Drafters	80,000
Bank officers and managers	75,000
Insurance agents/brokers	69,750

directly from the Bureau of Labor Statistics. Consult your regional office for the current price and ordering instructions.

Boston
1603 Federal Building
Government Center
Boston, Massachusetts 02203

Chicago
9th Floor
Federal Office Building
230 South Dearborn Street
Chicago, Illinois 60604

Table 2.
FIELDS EXPECTED TO EXPERIENCE RAPID GROWTH

OCCUPATION	ESTIMATED NUMBER OF NEW JOBS
Industrial machinery mechanics	160,000
Emergency medical technicians	143,500
Air-conditioning/refrigeration/heating mechanics	87,500
Health service administrators	80,000
Sewer plant operators	50,000
Computer service technicians	25,000
Insulation workers	15,000
Dental hygienists	13,500
Marketing researchers	12,500
Occupational therapists	5,300

New York
Suite 3400
1515 Broadway
New York, New York 10036

Philadelphia
P.O. Box 13309
Philadelphia, Pennsylvania 19101

Atlanta
1371 Peachtree Street N.E.
Atlanta, Georgia 30309

Dallas
2nd Floor
555 Griffith Square Building
Dallas, Texas 75202

Kansas City
911 Walnut Street
Kansas City, Missouri 64106

San Francisco
450 Golden Gate Avenue
Box 36017
San Francisco, California 94102

Determining Your Career Preferences

There are two steps to this exercise.

1. Think about and list those jobs and careers that you have, at one time or another, considered.

2. Rank these careers according to the income needs you came up with in Chapter 4.

Your Career/Job List

In the following spaces, list the various jobs and careers that you have ever seriously considered. Be as general or as specific as you like; describe the job or career if you don't know the proper name for it. The order in which you write them down is unimportant; you'll do your rankings in the second half of the exercise.

1. _____
2. _____
3. _____
4. _____
5. _____
6. _____
7. _____
8. _____
9. _____
10. _____
11. _____
12. _____
13. _____
14. _____
15. _____

How many could you think of? Ten? Fifteen? In our experience, most people have trouble coming up with more than ten careers that they have seriously considered—and this includes those job seekers who claim to have no specific idea what they are looking for. The fact is that most people, even those who don't think they know what they want, have a pretty good idea of their capabilities and their tastes. However, until they are asked to stop and think about their choices, they tend to confuse their own tastes with those of their friends, parents, co-workers, official and unofficial advisors, and so forth. It's also easy to get confused by the barrage of information that comes at us all day and all night long from the various media—it's no wonder we're confused, even if we actually do have a pretty good idea what we want.

Have you left anything off your list or included anything which is clearly absurd? Can you think of any jobs or careers related to the ones you've listed that you might also enjoy? If you feel hampered by your lack of knowledge of the current employment situation, *now* is the time to look through the *Occupational Outlook Handbook*. (You might also take a look at the want ad section of your local newspaper—more on that later.) Remember, taking a little time now can save a lot of time later.

The Rankings

Do you remember your income priorities from Chapter 4? Write them down again; if your priorities have changed since then, you should update them.

The next step is to see how your occupational choices and your income priorities relate to each other. The rating system is quite simple. Under each of the five income categories, you will list *in descending order* your career choices that can best fulfill that income requirement. A career choice may appear only once in each income category, but it can be in any position within that category. Rating points are noted on the right side of each line. For example, Delia Garcia's income priorities went as follows:

1. Security

2. Meet people

3. Money

4. Fulfillment

5. Identity

Her occupational choices (she could only think of eight) were as follows:

1. Bank officer

2. Outside sales person

3. Dental assistant

4. School guidance counselor

5. Secretary

6. Personnel counselor

7. Assistant to eye doctor

8. Arts administrator

Her rankings were as shown below.

DELIA GARCIA'S CAREER RANKINGS

			Scale low	high
INCOME No. 1:	Security			
Career No. 1:	Bank officer		(15)	(20)
2:	Dental assistant		(13)	(18)
3:	Eye doctor assistant		(12)	(17)
4:	Secretary		(11)	(16)
5:	School guidance counselor		(10)	(15)

INCOME No. 2:   Meet people

Career No.   1:   Arts administrator   (12)

              2:   Outside salesperson   (11)

              3:   Personnel counselor   (10)

              4:   Bank officer   (9)

              5:   Eye doctor assistant   (8)

INCOME No. 3:   Money

Career No.   1:   Outside salesperson   (10)

              2:   Dental assistant   (9)

              3:   Eye doctor assistant   (8)

              4:   Bank officer (beginner)   (7)

              5:   Secretary   (6)

INCOME No. 4:   Fulfillment

Career No.   1:   Arts administrator   (9)

              2:   School guidance counselor   (8)

              3:   Personnel counselor   (7)

              4:   Bank officer   (6)

              5:   Secretary   (5)

INCOME No. 5:   Identity

Career No.   1:   Arts administrator   (8)

              2:   Bank officer   (7)

              3:   School guidance counselor   (6)

              4:   Personnel counselor   (5)

              5:   Eye doctor assistant   (4)

Although Delia had rated "security" her number-one income choice, she didn't consider it to be of significantly more importance to her than her other choices; therefore, she went with the low scale when she did her arithmetic. Her occupational rankings are shown below.

DELIA GARCIA'S OCCUPATIONAL CHOICES

Position	Occupation	Points
1	Bank officer	44
2	Eye doctor assistant	32
3	Arts administrator	29
4	School guidance counselor	24
(tie) 5	Dental assistant	22
(tie) 5	Secretary	22
(tie) 5	Personnel counselor	22
6	Outside salesperson	21

We will discuss Delia Garcia's occupational choices—why she made them and how she acted upon them—in a moment. First, it's time for you to make your choices. Indicate your choices on the following blank form. If, in any of the income categories, you feel that your present career or position fulfills the requirements, simply write "stay."

CAREER RANKING CHART

		Scale	
		low	high
INCOME No. 1:*	_____		
Career No. 1:	_____	(15)	(20)
2:	_____	(13)	(18)
3:	_____	(12)	(17)
4:	_____	(11)	(16)
5:	_____	(10)	(15)

*The top income priority, Income No. 1, is, for some people, of far greater significance than their other income choices. If this is true for you, use the high point scale. If your top income priority is only marginally more significant to you than the others, use the low scale.

INCOME No. 2: _____

Career No.   1: _____ (12)

                2: _____ (11)

                3: _____ (10)

                4: _____ (9)

                5: _____ (8)

INCOME No. 3: _____

Career No.   1: _____ (10)

                2: _____ (9)

                3: _____ (8)

                4: _____ (7)

                5: _____ (6)

INCOME No. 4: _____

Career No.   1: _____ (9)

                2: _____ (8)

                3: _____ (7)

                4: _____ (6)

                5: _____ (5)

INCOME No. 5: _____

Career No.   1: _____ (8)

                2: _____ (7)

                3: _____ (6)

                4: _____ (5)

                5: _____ (4)

Do your arithmetic. Remember to select either the high or low scales for Income No. 1 and enter the results below.

Position	Occupation	Points
1	_____	____
2	_____	____
3	_____	____
4	_____	____
5	_____	____

Analyzing the Results

Are you surprised by the results, or did the career rankings turn out the way you expected them to? In a test group of job applicants who did this exercise, over half of the respondents were surprised by the results. Delia Garcia's reaction was typical; she was shocked and dismayed by her career ratings.

Why? Because the results frightened her—she did not like the order of her career choices. We had long talks with her and others whose responses were similar. What we learned is that although they had filled in both their income choices and Career Ranking Preference Charts in good faith, the results raised grave doubts about their choices. Delia Garcia explains:

I was very unhappy when I saw the results of the exercise because I really have no interest in being a bank officer or an assistant to an eye doctor (or optometric assistant, as it's properly called). I only put them on my list because I have one close friend who is a bank executive and another who is an optometric assistant. Both of them were about my age (mid-30s) when they started their careers; both are very happy with their work. In fact, all the careers I listed, except for arts administrator, are careers that friends and acquaintances have and are happy with. And all of them, like me, tried many different jobs before really starting their careers. I suppose that I unconsciously calculated that these careers were open to someone in my position, while other careers might not be.

That was my first mistake. My second mistake was my choice of income priorities. When I filled out the income questionnaire, it seemed perfectly logical to start with "security." Looking back on it, I'd say that was a dumb choice. My husband has a fine job, we own a house, we have a little money saved. I *have* security, or at least as much security as anyone has nowadays. What I really want is to get out of the house, to do something in the world, to meet interesting people, to feel like I'm accomplishing something.

I've always had a strong interest in the arts, and I know that there are organizations such as galleries and foundations that deal with the arts on a day-to-day basis—and, of course, there are people who administer these organizations. I guess I was secretly hoping that my "arts administrator" choice would end up with the highest rating, but it's obvious why it didn't.

I see now that my income choices were off-base, which is why my career choices came out the way they did. If I had placed "fulfillment," or "identity," or even "meet people" in first, second, and third places, "arts administrator" would have easily scored the highest number of points.

My income choices seem so odd to me now that I see where they lead. I don't want to be a bank officer or any of those other things. I want to find a job in an arts organization.

Of course, there were those respondents whose results came as a pleasant surprise to them. There was one young man whose parents, not unlike those of Scott Lehman, had been pushing him all his life to join them in their business, a retail clothing shop. When we first spoke with him, he didn't know what he wanted to do; his parents' business was just one option among countless others. When he set those options down on paper, however, he realized that there really weren't so many after all; and when he completed the career preference exercise and did the arithmetic, he discovered that, according to his own calculations, his parents' business was the place for him after all. When he went to work with them, it was with the conviction that he was making his own decision. (Needless to say, there was no agency commission on that particular placement. Oh well, win some, lose some.)

And then there were those who were not surprised by the outcome of the exercise. In general, these applicants had taken care in choosing their income preferences and had given a lot of thought to their potential occupational choices; the exercise served to confirm choices they had already made rather than to give them new ideas.

Finally, there were those whose highest rating went to "stay," which means that they had given their highest rating to what they were already doing. For those who didn't like their current position, this was very disconcerting and usually led them to revise their income requirements. To others it was reassuring; it convinced them that they had either already made the right career decision or they had gotten lucky and fallen into a career that suited them. These, we should add, constituted a distinct minority.

What about you? Are you satisfied with the way your ratings turned out? If the top choice reflects what you feel is your true career direction, then your income choices and your career choices are in sync, and all that remains to be determined is how closely attuned your choices are to the needs of the economic community around you. If your second and third choices also represent careers that you feel ready to undertake, all the better—flexibility is always an asset.

But if you, like Delia Garcia, are worried about your top-rated career, then it's time to review the thinking that led up to that rating.

- Do your income choices truly represent what you want or only what you think you ought to want? If what you really want is to spend all your time outdoors but you selected "medical plan" as your top income priority, you'd better go back and rethink the whole thing.

- Are your occupational choices realistic and in tune with your income needs? Are you just guessing about careers? You probably need more information about real-world career possibilities. Chapters 11 and 12 will help you find that information.

Embarking on a career that you don't like from the outset is no way to go. Taking a job to fulfill needs that you don't really have is absurd. Even if you don't feel compelled to enter a specific field, by now you ought to know, if only by a process of elimination, which ones hold some fascination for you. It is better to be warm than neutral. Remember, getting on the inside of an occupation opens up a whole new perspective; and getting on the inside of one about which you are optimistic gives direction to your enthusiasm and shape to your career plans.

Deciding on a Career

Are you satisfied with the results of the Career Ranking Chart? If so, your next step is obvious; decide to get a job you'll like in the field of your choice! Part Two of the book, starting with the following chapter, will guide you through the job hunt.

What to do if you're not satisfied with your Career Ranking Chart results? Chances are

- You need more information about the job marketplace.

- Your priorities aren't clear enough.

- You don't visualize your assets clearly enough.

- Your overall goals are undeveloped.

- You're not quite ready to take the leap into the marketplace.

- Any combination of the above.

Speaking first of priorities, visualization of assets, development of goals, and readiness to leap, we suggest looking back over the ground we have already covered. We're certain that, if you've done all the exercises and filled in all the charts, you'll find some clues to your priorities, capabilities, and goals. Your readiness to leap is really a function of feeling comfortable with yourself and your ability to make a decision and carry it through.

If you're still uncertain, it would probably help to talk it over with someone else. In addition to finding an advisor (which is discussed in Chapter 11), it might be useful to find an employment counselor now who could guide you through the job hunt process. (See the Employment Agency section of Chapter 12.)

Your advisors and employment counselors can also provide a wealth of information about the job marketplace if it's information you lack. Local want ads, of course, are a key to the local employment situation. Speaking to just about anyone currently employed in a field that remotely interests you will highlight that field; if they don't have the information you need, they'll probably be able to tell you who does.

The key once again is to make a decision and act on it, even if the decision at this point is only to speak with someone who might have some information for you. What if you have come to the conclusion that your first decision must be to get more experience or more education?

More Experience

It's a big step to recognize that in order to reach your ultimate career goal, you need to get more experience; you now have a very clear sense of direction and an obvious short-term goal. After you have decided upon the type of job you need to gain this experience—and it may take some research to discover what type of job that is—we suggest you put all your energy into finding and landing that job. Don't be distracted by your long-range goals; after all, the short-range goal is in the service of the long-range goals. And don't be depressed that the job you are applying for isn't the job of your dreams. If you really need the experience and if your long-range goals are worthwhile, then a "stepping stone" job is very important indeed. Remember—after you have determined that you need more experience, getting a job that will give you that experience should become your top priority.

Another way to gain experience, especially valuable for those with limited contact with the marketplace, is to work as a temporary for a while. Chapter 10 contains a full discussion of this increasingly popular way to gain experience and income at the same time.

More Education

College Degrees

Contrary to information being promulgated by certain employment counselors, there are some occupations for which no amount of positive thinking is enough to get you where you want to go. No one ever got to be a doctor simply by writing the perfect résumé, and there are few dentists, accountants, engineers, scientists, or lawyers who entered their professions as a result of knowing what style of clothing to wear to an interview. Without the proper educational background, these professional careers are strictly off limits.

That's the bad news. The good news is that, now more than ever before, it is possible to get the degree you need to enter the profession of your choice. All you have to do is make up your mind to do it and devise a plan to make it possible.

Declining undergraduate enrollment throughout the 70s forced most colleges and universities to reevaluate their admissions policies or risk fiscal oblivion. In addition to attempting to make their institutions more appealing to high school students bound for college, admissions officers discovered the "adult" student—the individual who hadn't been inside a classroom in two years or twenty and who wished to continue with his or her education.

Institutions which had long considered their adult-education divisions to be novelty adjuncts to their regular credit-bearing programs suddenly started offering mature students the same course menus that previously had been enjoyed only by young, matriculated undergrads. Professors began to discover that many of their adult-division students were sharper, worked harder, and provided a more stimulating atmosphere than younger, less experienced students. Almost overnight, teaching adult-education courses changed status from being a moonlighting activity for teachers, done only for the extra money, to being a choice teaching assignment. The quality of teaching improved, the quality of students continued to improve, and the academic quality of adult divisions of most institutions began to match that of their undergraduate divisions.

Most adults face two major problems when considering going back to school: time and money. These, of course, are formidable problems, and we'd be lying if we told you not to give them a second thought. Fortunately, however, for anyone considering going back to school, these problems have been given much thought both by the educational institutions concerned and federal and state governments; every effort is being made to help you get the education you need.

Most institutions, for example, in anticipation of the adult student's time problems, have flexible scheduling that allows the student to attend days, nights, or weekends, and to take as many or as few courses as time allows. At most institutions, the cost per course is probably lower than you would expect, and many states have scholarship and loan programs available to the adult student. Obviously, the fewer courses you are taking at any one time, the smaller the financial bite. Under certain circumstances, educational expenses incurred to maintain or improve skills required by the individual in his or her present employment may be deductible for federal income tax purposes; education assistance under an employer's education plan may be considered nontaxable income as well. We recommend that you discuss these possibilities with an accountant or tax advisor.

If you are considering a career that requires a degree, don't let the lack of that degree stop you! *Now* is the time to take action, not ten years from now. Take twenty minutes to phone colleges, universities, and community colleges in your area. Ask about their adult programs, have them send you their literature, and—if this is what it takes to get you moving—make an appointment with the registrar for two or three days after you expect to get the literature. If you're one of the lucky ones whose present career received high ratings in the previous chapter and you're interested in advancing rather than changing careers, speak with your supervisor or boss to see what company policy is on education. You might be surprised; many companies that have educational programs don't say very much about it to their employees. And, even when there is no formal company policy on education, many companies will partially or fully support an employee's education if it's clear that 1. The education will help the employee do a better job for the company, and 2. The employee is not about to leave the company as soon as he or she completes the program.

And what about the time element? This, for most people considering going back to school, is the problem that seems insurmountable. How does one find time for school and studying while continuing to earn a living, take care of the family, and see one's friends occasionally? We spoke with a woman of forty-seven who has been in college for the past two years, studying to be a librarian.

The hardest part, really, was making the decision to go back to school. That took me seven or eight years. Actually, you could say I was making the decision to go back to school ever since the day I dropped out of college to get married.

I had no idea where I'd find the time. It wasn't as if I'd been sitting around the house doing nothing all those years—I was *busy* raising three kids, keeping the house together, taking part-time jobs when I felt up to it. I mean, I had no idea when I was going to find time to go to classes, much less to do homework. All I knew was the time had come, and I wasn't about to let anything stop me.

Before I enrolled, I must have spent two or three months preparing my husband and my youngest son, who was still at home at the time, for my "disappearance." I thought I would have to lock myself away for days at a time to get anything done, and I guess I felt guilty about it. *They* kept telling me not to worry about it, that I'd be fine, but I didn't believe it.

I was very nervous before I started classes, but by the end of the first day, I had too much to think about to be nervous. The best part was that I thought it would take me months to get back into the swing of being a student, but it didn't take long at all, maybe a week at the most.

I started out as a full-time day student, and I did that for about a year.

The main thing that suffered was my television watching; I went from maybe fifteen hours a week down to almost zero, and I didn't miss it a bit. In fact, I began to wonder how I'd ever found the time to watch it before. I had to be strict with my husband and my son, though. They weren't allowed to bother me while I was studying unless there was an emergency, which made them more aware of what goes on around the house. They both became excellent shoppers and cooks and mediocre dishwashers.

In my second year, I decided to take a part-time job, drop one class, and see what happened. I surprised myself—as my work load increased, so did my grades. The discipline I had developed the year before served me well; I hardly ever felt pressured for time, and I even had time to relax on the weekends and go out once, sometimes twice, a week with my husband.

Am I glad I made the decision? My only regret is that I waited so long—it was the best decision I ever made.

So, if you are dissatisfied with your present life and feel that the only way out is to get your degree, don't hesitate! Start doing your research now. Thousands of adults every year make the decision to go back to school, and you're every bit as qualified as they are.

Proprietary Schools

Proprietary or privately owned schools teach everything from bartending to truckdriving, from typing to poodle grooming. Courses may only be a day or two long, or they may run two years or longer. If what you need is not a degree but specific skill training, you might find what you need at a proprietary school rather than at a college or university.

Every metropolitan area has a number of proprietary schools; in many cities there are several schools specializing in the same curricula and competing for the same students. Should you enroll in a proprietary school? And if so, how do you know which one to choose?

If it is clear to you that you need a specific skill or set of skills to help launch your career, then you should let nothing stop you from acquiring those skills. What you have to determine is if the skills can best be acquired on the job or by taking a course; the best way to make your determination is to speak with someone in the field—*not* someone in the proprietary school business. Asking someone in the school business is like asking a stereo sales person if you ought to buy a new system—a sales pitch is guaranteed.

If it turns out the skill you need must be acquired before you enter your field, it's time to start shopping for a school. Give yourself some time to come to your decision about a school; better to spend the time now than waste it later in a course that doesn't do you any good. In many subjects, proprietary schools compete with local colleges and universities for students. Before you sign up with a proprietary school, make sure you've investigated the public institutions in your area as well; they are sometimes less expensive than privately owned schools.

This isn't to imply that all proprietary schools are unscrupulously operated; on the contrary, many of them have outstanding reputations. However, as with any industry, there are always a few bad apples. Don't take anything for granted. The state agencies that are responsible for policing proprietary schools are often understaffed; inspectors are often overworked and unprepared in the subject matter of the schools they inspect. Follow these rules when choosing a proprietary school.

1. Don't even think about enrolling in a proprietary school unless you decide that you need a specific skill or skills to help you meet a career objective. Many people are lulled into signing up for a proprietary school program by the advertised promise of a terrific career. That's fine—for *them*. Remember, you are methodically playing out your own career scenario; you'll sign up for a course because you need it—when you need it.

2. When you visit a proprietary school for the first time, you are not there to sign up; you are there to *meet* the people at the school, both staff and students, to see if they impress or distress you. You are there to get the full story about the course or courses that you need and to find out how the finances work. You are there to see if the facilities of the school meet your expectations, and you will insist on seeing the same classrooms and labs that you'll be using if

you become a student. Trust your first impressions; if the people or the facilities make you queasy, it's not the place for you. And even if you like the place, don't sign up until you've seen the other schools in your area which teach the same subjects.

3. Never succumb to a hard sell. The odds are good that the harder they're selling, the less they have to sell. This is a big decision you're about to make, a decision concerning your future; if the school is attempting to foist a program upon you like it's a used car, don't buy it! Some schools have been known to go so far in their sales efforts as to have solicitors on the street grabbing people and promising oodles of federal scholarship dollars and wonderful jobs upon graduation. If you are approached by such a solicitor, run!

4. Take the course you want and only that course. Don't be sold a bill of goods on a "total program," even if you are offered a special bargain price on a package. *You* are charting your career course, and it is up to *you* to decide what you need. Don't trust your decisions to those with vested interests. Don't be conned into thinking you need a special degree or certificate that is available only if you take a one- or two-year course. If you've determined that all you need is a two-week refresher course in typing, then that's what you need. Period!

5. Read the enrollment agreements of the schools you visit. Make sure that at the moment of signing up, you won't be hit with substantial hidden costs that catch you by surprise.

6. Assume that you or your employer, if you can swing it, and *not* the federal government will be picking up the tab for your course or courses. The government does, indeed, provide scholarship assistance for thousands of proprietary school students, but only if they are matriculated, full-time students in a one- or two-year course. This is not to suggest that these courses are worthless, only that they are usually not necessary for people who have a well-planned career strategy. Others, who have no sense of career direction, may benefit from a year or two of gratuitous schooling; *you,* on the other

hand, want to take your course, learn your skills, and get out into the real world. The few dollars you spend on your course are easier to get back than the time you might have wasted fulfilling meaningless requirements to meet the government's conditions.

Assuming that you go by these rules, your chances are excellent of finding a proprietary school where you can acquire the skills you need to get the job you want.

A Note to the Returnee

The biggest problem for many returnees is summoning up the confidence to take the first step. What we recommend is to start immediately to talk with employment counselors, proprietary or university registrars, corporate personnel people—anyone who might give you informed feedback on how you could best fit in with the local employment scene. Talking with these people will build your confidence; you'll find more often than not that they're as interested in your point of view as you are in theirs.

As we've said, the returnee today is regarded as a precious commodity on the employment market. Your maturity and judgment are sought after, as well as your dependability and your ability to get along with others. Whether you have a clear-cut career direction or a generalized desire to get out of the house and into the world, we think you'll be surprised at how warmly you'll be greeted by counselors and potential employers alike.

While younger job hunters often spend months trying to find a job that is "just right," returnees are known for their ability to recognize a good position when it presents itself without wasting time comparing it with every other available position in town. The mature job seeker, being a veteran decision maker, is capable of having his or her career (or second career) decisively underway in a remarkably short time.

Incidentally, many returnees are getting back into the swing of things by working as temporaries for a number of weeks or months before deciding to go after a full-time position. Some of our older temporaries enjoy it so much that they've actually turned down full-time job offers.

We'll only say it once more—don't hesitate. Make the decision and take the step. You won't regret it.

PART TWO

SETTING YOUR CAREER IN MOTION

7

PACKAGING YOURSELF

Employers, supervisors, bosses all have a sixth sense about them; they know within the first two days whether a new employee is in full possession of the fundamentals that constitute an able worker. But what do they look for in someone who has not yet been hired, someone who is applying for a job?

Applying for a job is not unlike presenting a gift to someone; *you* are the gift and the presenter, the organization to which you are applying is the recipient. The idea is to get them to open the gift, which means hiring you. Before they hire you, the only thing they have to go by is your *packaging*. If it's attractive, they'll probably want to see what's inside; if it's not attractive, they're not going to be interested in seeing more.

There are five elements of personal packaging.

Your credentials
Your speech
Your dress
Your personal hygiene
Your attitude

Each one is important; and when they are all working together, your packaging is irresistible.

Credentials

Your credentials are, essentially, everything about you that can be written down on paper that is of interest to a potential employer. Your résumé is really nothing more than a specific format for listing your credentials. (See Chapter 8 for more on résumés.) The word *credential* comes from the Latin root meaning "belief," as in *credibility*. Credentials, in other words, are what make you believable. Anyone can walk in off the street and apply for a job; your credentials help convince the employer that you are for real, that you can do the job, that you are believable.

There are three major types of credentials.

Personal Credentials

These include recommendations from friends, current or former employers, current or former teachers, and anyone else who is in a position to comment (positively, we would hope) on you and who him- or herself possesses some credibility. If you can get a personal recommendation from someone who knows both you and the person to whom you are presenting the recommendation, all the better.

Academic Credentials

High school diplomas, college and graduate degrees, certificates from business or trade schools all represent academic credentials. Academic credentials represent different things to different employers. The Wall Street lawyer might be most interested in whether you went to an Ivy League law school; the personnel director of the advertising agency might be interested in seeing your business school certificate that says you can type eighty-five words per minute. In general, academic cre-

dentials represent your ability to finish a project that you have started
(that is, law school, college, high school, or a two-week typing course).

Occupational Credentials

These constitute your list of career accomplishments to date: the way
you saved your employer $100,000 a year for the past five years by
your advanced security procedures; the way your department's sales
have been increasing every year since you've been with the company;
the way you revamped the catalogue system at your college library;
the fact that you edited your high school newspaper; the way you were
able to raise six kids and be a part-time insurance salesperson. These
are the credentials, generally, that fill up résumés.

Everyone has credentials—you can't be without credentials any more
than you can be without any weather; there's always something to be
said about where you've been and what you've done. Those who think
they don't have any credentials are either very young, in which case
they are not expected to produce a five page résumé, or homemakers
returning to the work force after a long absence, which is a big credential in itself, if presented properly. What's important is to make
sure that your credentials are telling the right story. Mentioning that
you were a camp counselor might mean nothing to an employer; but
saying that you were in charge of a group with eight counselors and
forty screaming seven-year-olds under you—that's another story.

Speech

There are lots of stories about the panic that hit Hollywood when the
talkies were first introduced. Actors and actresses who were superstars
in the silent era saw their popularity plummet instantly upon the release
of their first talking pictures; others who were minor stars suddenly
were elevated to supernova status because they could *talk*. The entire
motion picture business was turned upside down, and all because of
sound.

We recently witnessed an event that reminded us of the importance of good speech. A young man came to Career Blazers as a job applicant. He filled out his application form and handed it in to a counselor. The young man was handsome, well dressed, and had fine credentials—on paper. The counselor took him into her office, whereupon the applicant looked around, smiled a charming smile, and said, "Eyy, dis a pretty neat lookin' office you got, you know? You tink you's gonna find me a job?"

For better or worse, you are judged by the way you talk. Perhaps, if you are interested in a career where you don't have to deal with other people, you can get along with sloppy English. But if you are considering a career in which you'll have any dealings at all with other people, you'd better pay attention to the way you speak because your speech is one of the first personal attributes that any potential employer has contact with. Don't let it be the last.

If you think you may have a problem with your speech, don't run from it. Correcting speech problems can usually be accomplished far more easily with an objective advisor than by yourself; it is your job to find an advisor and get to work. Most cities have speech therapists that are listed in the telephone book, but you may be able to solve your problem by working with your advisor, developing your ear, and practicing.

The way you talk is at least as important to your career development as any of the other elements of your package, and there are those who would assert that your speech is your most important single attribute because with a golden tongue, it is possible to explain away a host of shortcomings that might otherwise prove a hindrance to your employment. So don't get caught with your "dems" and "does" showing!

Dress

There have been a number of "dressing for success" books published recently, most of which contain reasonably astute observations about the relationship between how you dress and how your career is or is not progressing. Suffice it to say that clothing is important, and anyone who tells you otherwise is living in a dream world.

There is no universal right way to dress; what's right is what is appropriate for the particular occupation, season, location, and so forth. In most fields (exceptions would be those such as the music business, where bizarre dress is *de rigueur*), there is no way to impress a potential employer with your clothing. In other words, your clothing should read good taste, but not in a pushy way; it should not take an interviewer's mind off the interview. All deviations from a good, tasteful, solid, successful neutral—whether these deviations are in the direction of high fashion or punk—read *negative* to your interviewer or your current employer, for that matter.

First impressions are telling, and your clothing is usually the first thing about you that anyone will notice. It doesn't pay to alienate people—especially potential employers—in that first split-second, does it? Pay attention to the way others in your field, or your intended field, dress. Don't ignore your own taste; just make sure it is applied to clothing that is in the right ball park. And if you find that the more you try to figure out how to dress, the more baffled you become, by all means go back to your bookstore and find a book that tells you all about how to dress. Don't let your wardrobe hold you back!

Personal Hygiene

This one may seem a little, well, *personal,* but if we don't mention it, who will? If there is any laxity in your personal hygiene, it probably will not be noticed as quickly as wardrobe deficiencies or speech foibles, but it will certainly leave the most indelible impression.

Don't be sabotaged by sloppy habits. Bathe or shower frequently. Wash your hair frequently—with an antidandruff shampoo if necessary. Greasy hair and dandruff are probably the most apparent of all hygiene problems. You may not pay attention to such things, but take our word for it—everyone else does! Make sure your clothes are clean and pressed, your shoes shined, your fingernails clean and trimmed. If you need deodorant or a deodorant soap, use them. If you're in doubt, use them! These are all easy problems to solve; not to make the small effort involved is to deliberately quash your own career plans.

There are other problems, such as skin and weight problems, which may be perceived as hygiene problems although they are actually medical problems. We strongly urge you to seek medical attention for such conditions *before* you start your job search in earnest. It may be unfair, but it is a fact of life; an unhealthy appearance can diminish your chances of getting hired for the job you want.

Attitude

Attitude, in a sense, includes all the other elements of your personal packaging; everything may be considered an expression of your attitude. But there is another facet of attitude—it could be called your *behavior*—that is separate from your other packaging elements, and that can negate all the positive effects of the other elements if it is not pointing in the right direction.

We guarantee that your attitude will be tested in every job interview you ever take, even in the interviews you have with counselors at personnel agencies. The questions may vary from one interview to the next, but the intent is the same—to determine if you are capable of contributing to a team effort. This doesn't just mean doing your work, coming in on time, dressing properly, etc. It means bringing with you a positive energy that makes others enjoy working with you—good vibes, if you will.

Obviously, there is no way for interviewers to determine how you'll do in combat conditions without actually hiring you and finding out. What they can do, however, is to ask leading questions designed to bring your attitude to the surface. For example, questions about the interviewee's current boss or supervisor will sometimes lead to bitter, acrimonious responses; this is a tip-off to the interviewer that he is speaking with someone who does not get along with authority figures. (Chapter 13 will go into depth on interviews.)

Attitude isn't something that can be put on like clothing or makeup; it is an inherent part of your personality, although it can be changed over a period of time if you're willing to work at it. In our opinion, the key to a winning attitude is enthusiasm for your work or, in an interview situation, enthusiasm for the work you hope to be doing for that employer. Enthusiasm comes when you feel that your job is an important element in your overall career plan; you feel that you are working for *yourself,* and therefore you are enthusiastic. Enthusiasm also comes from the day-to-day pleasure you take in doing your job well and from working toward a common goal with a group of motivated co-workers. This may not sound anything like the job you now have, but it is up to you to do your part to make it so.

Don't let your attitude problems get the better of you. If you think you are communicating a lot of negative information, do something about it! Work with an advisor if necessary; do practice interviews with friends and family members; run fifteen miles a day if that's what it takes to purge the negativity, but purge it. It's your own career that will suffer if you don't.

Start thinking about your packaging now, not the night before your first big interview. If you think you need to work on some of your packaging elements, start working on them now. Twenty minutes or a half-hour a day spent in solving these relatively simple problems will pay off with big dividends later on in your career program.

RÉSUMÉS

Every day's crop of job applicants brings with it a varied collection of résumés, and every day we are surprised at the extent to which people are confused about the function of a résumé. On the one end of the scale, we see résumés that we call "great American novels"— fifteen or twenty pages of autobiographical flotsam and jetsam, bound in a fancy cover, with a glossy photo of the applicant on the frontispiece; on the other end of the scale, we get scraps of loose-leaf paper containing scribbled notes on the applicant's employment record. It is a true test of our diplomatic skills when we have to tell the creators of these *oeuvres* that while we are not unappreciative of their intentions, we would under no circumstances consider actually forwarding their résumés to any of the organizations with which we do business.

We will now state in one sentence everything you'll ever need to know about the function of a résumé:

The function of a résumé is to get you an interview.

Résumé Presentation

Résumés are written for a very specific audience: potential employers. In smaller organizations, this could be the owner of the company; in larger organizations, it will usually be the director of personnel or someone else in the personnel department. Often, if you are applying for a specialized position, your résumé will also be read by your potential departmental supervisor. These people are usually very busy, and much of their time is spent reading résumés. Your résumé is not the first one they've ever seen, nor will it be the last. They know what they are looking for in a résumé and, what's more important, what they are *not* looking for. Résumés have a simple language all their own. Learn the language and you'll be guaranteed a second reading; don't learn the language, and you may as well save yourself the cost of paper.

An experienced personnel director can open your envelope, scan your résumé for "automatic no's," crumple it up, and toss it into the circular file within thirty seconds. If your résumé is to be effective, it must be free of automatic no's, and it must deliver its message clearly, unambiguously, and quickly.

Many people are put off by our list of résumé do's and don't's; they want their résumés to reflect their creativity and feel that an ordinary résumé will make them look like everyone else. Once again, however, you must try to see it from the other side of the desk. If you had to read perhaps fifty résumés before lunch every day, you, too, would be annoyed at those that didn't get right to the point or were hard to read. If you were reading quantities of résumés, you'd realize that green paper, pink paper, blue paper—every color except white or off-white—is hard on the eyes. This is not a matter of taste but a matter of fact. While you may think that your choice of purple paper distinguishes you from the pack, your reader is thinking, "That's one less résumé I have to read today." Crumple.

From time to time, someone in the employment advice field will come up with a brilliant new style of résumé guaranteed to have employers throwing money at you. These brilliant inventions are usually no more than variations on one or another résumé style that has been around for years—old wine in a new bottle. There really is no secret formula for résumé writing other than to be clear and concise. Anyone who tells you otherwise is leading you on.

Your résumé must identify and describe you.

You *must* include:
 Your name, address, and telephone number
 Description of your work history
 Professional licenses
 Publications, if any
 Membership in professional organizations
 Description of your educational background
 Academic honors, if any

You *may* include:
 Job objective or career goal
 Capsule description of work history
 Hobby information
 Willingness to travel or relocate
 Military service or draft status
 Statement of health
 Personal data: marital status and number of children; your
  age, height, weight, etc.

You must *never* include:
 Reasons for leaving past jobs
 Past salaries or present salary requirements
 A photograph of yourself
 Name of spouse or children
 Names and addresses of references

In addition, you must avoid automatic no's such as:
 An odd or unattractive résumé
 The use of strange colored paper (anything other than white
  or off-white) or cheap-looking paper
 A strange format (no more than two pages)

With very few exceptions, no résumé should be longer than two pages. For many, one page is sufficient. You definitely will *not* impress your reader with a longer résumé, and you may end up on the reject pile on the basis of length alone. Top corporate executives can tell their stories in two pages; there is no reason why you cannot.

Our focus will be on the two most widely used résumé styles: the historical or chronological résumé, and the functional résumé. Other styles come into fashion one season and look dated the next; by sticking with these "classics," you'll never go wrong.

Further Notes on Résumés

Type Your Résumé

It should go without saying, but we are constantly surprised at how many people still don't know that *you should never present a handwritten résumé*. All résumés should be typed, preferably on a good electric typewriter. If you do not have access to such a machine, don't be stingy; take your handwritten résumé to a professional typist (look in the Yellow Pages under "Typing Services") or to a résumé service (more on these later on in the chapter). A résumé that has not been typed has a maximum life expectancy of no more than two seconds in the hands of a professional résumé reader.

Reproducing Your Résumé

At one time, employers expected all résumés to be individually typed. Fortunately, those days are over; the modern duplication methods of photocopying and offset printing provide acceptable copies that are neat, clean, and cheap. Do not submit carbon copies or mimeographed copies, however; these techniques are sloppy and unacceptable. If you choose to have your résumé photocopied, you may have to sample a number of photocopy shops until you find one in your area that keeps its machine in clean running order. A well-maintained photocopy machine can produce copies that look as good as or better than original typed copy, but a poorly maintained machine will produce sloppy copies.

When reproducing your résumé, by whatever process, select a high quality paper, preferably a watermarked bond. The paper used ordinarily by quick printers and photocopy shops is of a low grade and frequently contains imperfections that can mar the appearance of your résumé. Don't balk at the expense of a high-grade paper; it will be minimal, and the effect it creates will far outweigh the small price you will pay for it. Once again, choose a white or off-white paper; any other color is strictly unacceptable for a résumé.

Sample Résumés

The Historical or Chronological Résumé

This résumé style presents your information not in ordinary chronological order but in *reverse* chronological order, starting with the most recent data and moving backwards. Dates are displayed either in a vertical column set to the side of the text or as a separate line that begins the body of the text. We have seen résumés where the dates are included in the body of the text, but, as time is of the essence in chronological résumés, they tend to disappear this way, and we do not recommend it.

Education is treated in the same manner as employment history; your most advanced degree is given first, followed in reverse order by other degrees and certificates. Academic honors may be included in this grouping.

If you choose to include your job or career objective, do so at the very beginning, after your name and address but before your employment history. Any other information, required or optional, should go at the very end.

Although, as a rule, the chronological résumé begins with your most recent experience, whether it be work or education, there is a special circumstance where this rule should be broken. If you have recently secured a college or graduate degree by going to school at night while working in your current field during the day and if your degree prepares you for work in a new field, then by all means start with your educational history (after your name and address, that is). If, however, you have recently obtained a degree that does not prepare you for a change of fields, then you are better off sticking with the original plan of putting your work history first. The key is to give prominence to whatever is most descriptive of your talents and abilities with the emphasis on your most *marketable* talents and abilities.

Most people will be able to fit their chronological résumés onto one page. Occasionally, if you have had a long career, your résumé will go on to a second page, but *in no case should it exceed two pages*. Even if you feel your history is so interesting that it demands a third or fourth page, stop at two. Remember—your reader wants just the facts.

See below for a sample of this type of résumé. The chronological résumé is, by far, the most popular and most effective résumé ever devised. If you are serious about your career, we strongly advise you to go with this format—it's the proven winner.

SAMPLE CHRONOLOGICAL RÉSUMÉ

John Feagin
12 Birch Drive
Woodbine, New Jersey 07756
(201) 554-3398

Career Objective: The position of office manager with a
fast-growing smaller company in the Woodbine area.

Experience:

1978-Present   Office Manager, Delta Industrial Fasteners,
               Tenafly, New Jersey. Manage office with staff
               of twenty-three full-time employees. In-
               volved in all phases of office operations:
               work-flow procedures; act as liaison between
               staff and line personnel, analyze produc-
               tivity and work with upper management in
               deciding how to increase productivity where
               necessary. Handle all personnel problems
               including vacation scheduling, arranging
               interviews, hiring and training of all per-
               sonnel.

1971-1978   Administrator/Office Manager, Civic Center,
               Plainfield, New Jersey. Maintained and
               supervised bookkeeping and accounting
               records. Payroll, purchasing, check recon-
               ciliation, general ledger. Prepared peri-
               odic financial statements, reviewed budget,
               maintained accurate membership records;

handled enrollment of new members; prepared
calendar of events for affiliated groups.
Administered and executed all policies made
by executive board.

1969–1971   Sales Representative, Associated Gifts,
Melrose, New Jersey. Called on wholesalers,
chain and retail stores as representative
of manufacturer and importer of gifts and
novelty items. Traveled extensively
throughout northeastern United States. Set
up exhibits at numerous trade shows.

Education:

1966–1970   Rutgers University,
New Brunswick, New Jersey.
BA, 1970

1962–1966   Melrose High School,
Melrose, New Jersey.
Academic Diploma, 1966

The Functional Résumé

The functional résumé (see below) emphasizes your qualifications and
abilities in terms of your job titles and responsibilities. This résumé
style doesn't give your career history as does the chronological résumé; rather, it highlights the various areas of your employment experience with the most important skills, functions, and responsibilities
listed first. Dates are not considered important and are either listed
inconspicuously or not at all. Education is treated separately and, as
with the work history, dates may be omitted entirely.

SAMPLE FUNCTIONAL RÉSUMÉ

John Feagin
12 Birch Drive
Woodbine, New Jersey 07756
(201) 554-3398

Job Objective: A position with a fast-growing smaller
company that utilizes my managerial talents as developed
over the past eleven years.

Work Experience:

Office Manager/Administrator: Worked with two very different organizations as office manager and administrator.
Have overseen all aspects of work-flow procedure and
staff development, including bookkeeping and accounting;
purchasing; preparation of periodic financial statements;
preparation of productivity charts; development of solutions to productivity problems; personnel hiring and firing, scheduling, training; acted as liaison between
staff and line personnel. Responsible for 200 percent
increase in productivity in mailroom plus considerable
increases in other departments. Increased organizational
membership by 350 percent while cutting costs in membership department by 25 percent.

> Delta Industrial Fasteners,
> Tenafly, New Jersey
> 1978–Present
>
> Civic Center,
> Plainfield, New Jersey
> 1971–1978

Sales Representative: Increased territorial sales by
over 350 percent in less than eight months. Called on
wholesalers, chain and retail stores, focusing on developing new dealers and increasing sales with previous
ones. Traveled extensively throughout northeastern
states. Set up exhibits at numerous trade shows; rede-
signed trade show booth and increased efficacy of trade
show effort; new booth and techniques adopted throughout
territories in continental USA.

> Associated Gifts,
> Melrose, New Jersey
> 1969–1971

Education:

BA 1970, Rutgers University
Attended London School of Economics in Junior Year
   Abroad program.

<u>Personal:</u>

```
Born: October 3, 1948
Height: 5' 11"
Married, two children
```

The functional résumé has been described as the perfect vehicle for stating actual talents and areas of achievement, which we do not dispute. However, we have found that many employers distrust a résumé with no dates given, and some employers even distrust a résumé where the dates are given but hard to find. They feel, rightly or wrongly, that by not listing the dates clearly, the applicant is trying to hide something, such as long periods of unemployment. We therefore recommend that, should you choose to write a functional résumé for yourself, you include dates whenever possible to reassure the reader that nothing has been deleted and that no periods of time have been unaccounted for.

Other types of résumés do exist; occasionally they even get results. However, there is no position for which either the chronological or functional résumé is not eminently suited. If you insist on learning about other résumé styles or if you require further information on résumés in general, we modestly recommend the definitive résumé book *How to Write Better Résumés* by Adele Lewis, published by Barron's.

Résumé Services

In recent years, résumé services have been sprouting up all over the country. How can you tell a good résumé service from a bad one? Why should you go to a résumé service in the first place?

We should start out by saying that if there were no need for résumé services, there wouldn't be any résumé services. And if legitimate résumé services did not exist, then the entire business would have gone under long ago.

The résumé business is predicated on the existence of several distinct types of customers.

1. Those who don't know how to write a résumé

2. Those who don't have the time to write a résumé

3. Those who know how to write a résumé, have the time to do it, but want an extra measure of professionalism in their résumés

4. Those in the upper-income categories who need executive search assistance as well as résumé writing and distribution functions

Some résumé services are little more than typing services; you bring in a list of your current and former jobs and they type up the list. Other résumé services include a full line of functions, including investigating your employment and educational history; exploring alternatives in résumés and writing one or more that are suitable to the job or jobs you are seeking; writing one or more types of covering letters; reproducing résumés and covering letters on high-quality paper; and assisting you in selecting a target group of organizations to receive your résumé. A résumé from the former type of service can cost as little as five or ten dollars; a package from the latter type of service may run into hundreds of dollars.

Is it worth it? If a $250 résumé and covering letter package is instrumental in landing you an interview that leads to a $30,000-a-year position, then, of course, it's worth it—that $250 represents less than 1 percent of your first year's salary! By the same token, a five-dollar résumé that doesn't help you get any interviews is five dollars down the drain.

Why should you go to a résumé service in the first place when, supposedly, you now know all you need to know about writing a résumé? If you are a reasonably facile writer with access to a good typewriter and photocopy machine, there's no reason in the world why you shouldn't write your own résumé, provided that you *want* to write it. Some people, we have found, have a block against writing their own résumé; they'll spend weeks and weeks looking for reasons why they don't have the time to sit down and do it. If you fall into this category, then by all means you should investigate your local résumé services. Having a résumé is crucial to your search; you can't really get started without one. If that means paying for one, then you ought to start reaching for your wallet. And what if you have trouble writing *anything*? If you have an aversion to writing, then you'd better start looking into résumé services now because if you don't do it now, you'll probably just have to do it later.

How do you tell a good résumé service from a bad one? Unless you know people who have used a certain résumé service and can give you their firsthand account, you'll have to use your own judgment about the quality of the people and the quality of the résumés they produce. In your investigation, you should:

- See as many samples from each résumé service as they'll show you. A good résumé service will be prepared for this; in fact, they will be proud to show you their work. Usually, their résumés will be neatly bound in a loose-leaf or other binding; occasionally they will be framed and hung on the wall. If the person you are talking to has to go fishing around in his or her desk to find résumé samples, forget it! Compare the résumés you are shown with each other. Ask to see résumés for various job descriptions—preferably job descriptions that are very different from one another. If they all look the same, if a résumé for an accountant has the same language and format as the one for a copy editor, the chances are that the résumé service in question is not producing custom résumés but is mass producing them and changing the names at the top of the page. If they are mass producing résumés while charging for custom work, find another service.

- Compare the price structures of various résumé services in your community. Be distrustful of those that are either much more or much less expensive than the average. However, make sure you are comparing apples with apples; a résumé service that is actually no more than a typing service is going to be *much* less expensive than one that actually researches and writes résumés.

- Don't jump into anything. Survey the lay of the land; then decide what you need before you make a commitment. If you know your résumé is good and all you need is typing and reproduction, don't be talked into any extras. On the other hand, don't succumb to false economies. If you need help composing your résumé and covering letter, if you need help selecting the organizations to send them to, then find someone who can help you. It'll cost you, but not nearly so much as it costs to be stuck in a job you are sick of.

- Keep in mind what we have been telling you about résumés in this chapter. Even if you decide not to write your own, you'll be able to tell if a résumé service is for real or if they're faking it.

- All things being equal, go with a résumé service that has a track record rather than a brash newcomer. Newcomers in this business have a nasty habit of insisting that they have a revolutionary way to do résumés, a style that makes all the others look obsolete. What they don't mention is that the people who will be reading your résumé most likely went to the old school and have no use for newfangled résumés. Remember, the purpose of your résumé is to get you an interview, not a reputation as an innovator of résumés.

- Get all the financial information before you make a deal. This includes information on the base price of your résumé, the price of reproducing it, the price of high quality paper, the price of mailing if the service is taking care of that, plus equivalent information about your covering letter. If you think they're trying to put one over on you, leave!

Above all, remember that it is *your* résumé, that it must represent you properly; a résumé service that imposes strange formats or unusual styles on your résumé is doing you a disservice. A résumé service must be willing and able to present you in as professional and dignified a fashion as you would present yourself. It is your career that's on the line, not theirs.

9

PREPARING YOUR COVERING LETTER

A covering letter (see pages 116–117) should be enclosed whenever you send your résumé to a prospective employer. While it will rarely say anything not already detailed in your résumé, its enclosure is an act of courtesy and a sign of a serious and professional approach to job seeking, and it gives each employer you approach an indication of personal attention that would not be shown by the arrival of an unaccompanied résumé.

Regardless of the circumstances, your covering letter should be brief, limited to no more than four paragraphs and certainly no longer than one typed page. Unlike the résumé, a covering letter should never be reproduced; it should always be individually typed. The only exception to this rule is that you may have your covering letter reproduced if it is done on an automatic typing or word processing machine, which is available at many professional typing and résumé services. Letters thus reproduced look exactly like handtyped letters. Needless to say, your letter should look neat and conform to the standards of business correspondence.

You should make every effort to address your covering letters to a particular individual in the company by *name*, not by title. Many companies automatically sort out those letters not addressed by name before the personnel director (or whoever it is to whom the résumé ought to be addressed) even gets to look at them, the rationale being, "If this job seeker can't take the time to discover the name of our personnel director, then we sure as heck aren't going to take the time to read it!" The exception to this is when you are responding to an ad, in which case you should address the letter as indicated in the ad, even if nothing more than a box number is given. Do not try to guess the title (and certainly not the name!) of the person who will be receiving it—you'll only look foolish.

NOTE: If you do not know the title and name of the person to whom you should send your résumé, your best bet is to send it to someone high up in the corporate hierarchy—the chief executive officer (CEO), the president, or a divisional vice-president. The names of these individuals may be found in a book called the *Directory of Directors*, available at most public libraries. It's not a bad idea to send your résumé to one of these higher-ups even when you *do* know the name of the person lower down the ladder who will actually be making the hiring decision. With a little luck, the higher-up will read your résumé, clip a note to it saying that it looks interesting, and pass it down the line to the executive in charge of your prospective department. Your résumé, distinguished by having arrived by way of a corporate bigwig, is sure to get immediate attention. Remember—while submission of your résumé to more than one executive of a large organization may help your cause, multiple submissions of your résumé to a smaller organization will only cause confusion.

The first paragraph of your covering letter should tell why you are writing to that particular company. If it is in answer to an ad, you should so state and give the name and date of the publication where the ad appeared. If someone who is an employee of the company has suggested you apply, you should give the name, title or job category, and department where employed. If you are writing as part of your own mail campaign, you should explain in two or three lines why you are interested in working with that particular company.

The next one or two paragraphs should point out the important features of your résumé that could be of interest to your reader. These could be features in either your educational background or your work history. In some circumstances, you could elaborate slightly on one or two details of your résumé. For example, if your résumé simply states that you worked as circulation manager of a newspaper, your letter could add the information that the circulation increased by 40 percent in the six years you were there as a direct result of a program that you implemented. Again, be brief.

The last paragraph is your closing, indicating your hope that you have created interest in yourself and suggesting further communication to arrange an interview.

Using your covering letter to highlight certain aspects of your résumé allows you to use the same résumé for many different types of job opportunities. In addition, it personalizes the résumé, making it clear that you have not sent it out at random but have given some thought to its recipients.

A covering letter is not essential, as a résumé is. Nor can a good covering letter compensate for a bad résumé. However, we have found that, all things being equal, a résumé sent with a covering letter will tend to receive more attention than one sent without a covering letter. We urge you to include a covering letter with every résumé you distribute.

Additional information on covering letters is contained in *How to Write Better Résumés*.

SAMPLE COVERING LETTER: REPLY TO ADVERTISEMENT

88 Willow Way
Garden City,
New York 11530
July 5, 19—

Box 334X
New York *Globe*
454 West 52nd Street
New York, New York 10023

Dear Sir or Madam:

I am replying to your advertisement, dated July 4, 19—, offering a position as copy editor on a sports car publication.

As my résumé demonstrates, I have my BS in journalism and have been working as copy writer and assistant copy editor on magazines for the past six years.

Your ad specified an interest in and knowledge of sports cars. I did not feel it appropriate to mention it in my résumé, but I am the owner of one of the few surviving Type 57 Bugattis in North America, having restored and maintained the car myself. The car is registered with the Bugatti Club of America, to which I belong. I trust that this establishes my credentials as a sports car enthusiast.

If my background is of interest to you, please contact me at your convenience.

I appreciate your consideration.

Sincerely,

Raymond Shasta

Enc.

SAMPLE COVERING LETTER: DIRECT MAIL CAMPAIGN

338 Cresent Drive
Chicago, Illinois
60699
July 5, 19—

Mr. Aaron Lapthorpe
President
Seafarer's Museum
Windham, Maine 04453

Dear Mr. Lapthorpe:

I am applying for a position with your museum as I feel
my experience in developing a museum sales department
will be of interest to you.

As my résumé indicates, I held the position as sales
manager of Gotham Museum for six years. In this capacity, I developed a mail-order sales department and
created a successful bookshop specializing in native
handicrafts.

I expect to be in the vicinity of Windham the first week
of August. Could we set up an interview for that time?
As I am currently employed, I would appreciate that this
be kept in confidence.

I appreciate your consideration.

Sincerely yours,

Helene Lorimore

Enc.

10

DON'T QUIT YET

While the search for a new job or new career can be a lot of work, it should not be considered a full-time job in itself unless you are currently unemployed (which we'll discuss later on in this chapter). Why?

It is much easier to find a new job while you are still employed in your old job.

This doesn't mean it is easier to *look* for a job while you're still working at your current job; obviously, it's tough to be actively pounding the pavement and working in the office at the same time. What it means is that:

- From a potential employer's point of view, you are a more attractive applicant if you are currently employed.

- It's easier to enlist the aid of your current business contacts before you leave your job than it is after you leave your job.

If these two points seem strange, it's because they represent psychological truths of job hunting; we are just describing the way things are, not the way they ought to be. *You* know that you're the same person unemployed as you are employed, but potential employers don't always see it that way; all other factors being equal, they'll probably choose an employed person over an unemployed one. It's liable to be the same way with your business contacts and even with your friends, unfortunately. When you're employed, they're happy to recommend you; but when you're unemployed, the recommendations are harder to come by.

Therefore, unless you're on the verge of going completely insane in your current job, we strongly recommend that you do not quit until you secure a new position. If your heart's not in it, fake it. Think of it as one of the disciplines needed to get your career strategy in gear.

"READY ABOUT"

Making a turn in a sailboat is not like making a turn in a car—it's not a matter of simply pushing the rudder and turning. Before changing tack (direction), you must know which way the wind is blowing, the direction of the current, and how your sails are set. Then, before you actually start to turn, you must get going as fast as you can in your current direction—even if it's ninety degrees off your desired course—to build up the momentum you'll need to carry you and the boat through the turn.

It's a lot like this when you are changing jobs; the transition is smoother if you have good momentum going in your current job. One of the worst things you can do is to lose heart in your current job, withdraw your energy and interest, and start doing a sloppy job. Not only does this leave you feeling guilty, it makes it a lot harder to build up the momentum again in your new job. Furthermore, doing sloppy work in your current job can subtly undermine your self-confidence, which doesn't help you one bit in the interviews you'll be taking for a new position.

Before changing tack, the sailboat captain yells "Ready about!" to alert the crew to the upcoming change of direction. Before *you* change direction, you should alert yourself to the added pressures that a change of tack entails. Start building up your momentum now—it's hard to get it back once you lose it.

Avoid
Being Fired

"All right," you say. "I'm not going to quit, but what control do I have over whether or not I get fired?" Ultimately, of course, that control rests with your supervisor or boss. In some circumstances, such as a takeover of your company by another, your fate is totally out of your control, your dismissal a result not of your poor-quality work but of some corporate decision in a boardroom thousands of miles away.

However, in most situations, *you* are the one who determines whether or not you get fired. We have spoken with many thousands of individuals who have, at one time or another, been fired, and the overwhelming majority of them knew that something was up long in advance of their actual firing. Most of them, in fact, had been considering quitting; a majority said that they had lost interest in their job but were too timid or frightened to come right out and quit. Instead, they gradually withdrew their energies from their jobs until the boss had no choice but to fire them. In other words, *they* and not their bosses determined that they were to be fired; the boss was merely the agent of the firing.

Most supervisors and bosses hate to fire people; they consider it their most distasteful chore. Corporate policy in most organizations stipulates that no one is to be fired except in the most compelling circumstances. (This has more to do with unemployment insurance payments than with corporate beneficence, by the way.) Almost no one gets fired without warning, and often the warning signs start months, even years, in advance of the actual firing.

Warning Signs: Getting Fired

The following list details some of the warning signs indicating that you are on your boss's "hit list."

1. You are called to task by your boss or supervisor for a number of seemingly petty offenses such as being three minutes late, making a spelling error, taking a personal day without giving three weeks notice, making a small mistake on a petty-cash slip, or anything else that usually does not rate a discussion.

2. You are passed over for a raise or promotion.

3. You are not invited to a company meeting that you always attend.

4. Your shift has been changed.

5. After having lunch once a week with your boss or supervisor, he or she suddenly stops inviting you.

6. Through no request or desire of yours, you are shifted to a number of different positions within the company over the course of a few months.

7. You find that you are *not* being asked to do as much as you are accustomed to do.

Although these warning signs may seem ominous, they should not be taken as an indication of bad times ahead. On the contrary, if you are like most people, you began to lose interest in the job before the job began to lose interest in you; it's likely that you have been considering quitting but have been postponing action. Well, now's the time for action. If you are one of the few who love their jobs but are getting warning signs anyway, it's time you faced the fact that something's amiss.

What should you do if you've been getting warning signs? If you haven't already started to prepare a career strategy, start now. Buy yourself some time; work *hard* at your current job. Your boss or supervisor most likely will reconsider or postpone your dismissal when it becomes apparent that you are working harder than ever. This allows you to spend time looking for a new position without giving up your current one. Lastly, *don't* discuss the situation with your boss. A direct confrontation will often precipitate an action, which in this case means the possibility of your being fired or asked to resign on the spot. Your goal, remember, is to stall, to buy yourself time to find a new job—not to bring matters to a head.

Perhaps the most important advantage of keeping your current job while looking for a new one is dollars and cents. Believe it or not, there are people who are so eager to get away from their current jobs that they forget about money—money for rent, money for food, money for day-to-day necessities, and money for their job search. Having a résumé photocopied costs money, postage costs money, even newspapers cost money. There is nothing more depressing than being too poor to look for a job!

NOTE: It may sound strange, but your employer may suddenly take a second look at you once he or she knows that someone else is interested in hiring you. See "The Counter Offer" on page 175 of Chapter 14.

Out of Work?

What do you do if you are *already* unemployed? There's certainly no point in looking back to your last job, it's the future we're concerned with. As one of our counselors says, "When you're stuck with a lemon, make lemonade!" The one huge advantage to being unemployed is that you have lots of time to devote to your job search. Of course, the time is meaningless if you can't keep a roof over your head and if you are too depressed to sell yourself to potential employers. If you are currently unemployed, find a way to finance yourself until you find a new position. This may mean getting unemployment insurance if you are eligible, dipping into your savings, selling off your second car, or borrowing from a friend or family member who won't miss the money for a month or two. You might also consider taking a temporary or part-time position until you find a permanent one. (Temporary work is discussed in the next section.) In any case, it is essential that you have some form of financing ready to see you through until you find your new position. Otherwise, you may find yourself taking a job you don't really want—which puts you right back where you started.

Keep your spirits up. This may seem frivolous, but, believe us, it's not. We can always spot job applicants who are unemployed and upset about it—they walk through the door with a haggard, hangdog look; they are often unshaven and unshorn; they have no confidence in themselves in an interview. Sadly, it is these very people, the ones who would seem to need work badly, who have the hardest time finding a job; employers don't like to take on charity cases. How do you cure your unemployment blues?

1. Make sure your financial affairs are under control.

2. Make sure you spend several hours a day in a conscious, strategic effort to find your new position. If this means making up a schedule and sticking to it, then do it.

3. Consider taking up a physical activity, such as jogging, swimming, racketball, or anything else that is fun and active. It's crucial to keep your body in shape, especially if you are prone to depression because of your employment problems. Getting some exercise every day or every other day temporarily takes your mind off your problems, gives you a feeling of accomplishment, and makes you feel good about yourself.

Keeping yourself fit, healthy, and confident goes a long way toward offsetting the disadvantages of being an unemployed job searcher. In fact, quite a few of the unemployed people we have seen lately are in excellent job-hunting form and are able to present themselves to better advantage than are many unhappily employed applicants.

Working Temporary

There was a time, back in the '50s, when working as a temporary employee was frowned upon; it was assumed that you were a temporary because no one would hire you as a full-time employee. Fortunately, those days are ancient history; working temporary today is a respectable, useful, and sometimes even lucrative form of employment.

Temporary work is obtained through temporary personnel services, which can usually be found under "Employment Contractors" in the Yellow Pages. Temporary personnel services come in all shapes, sizes, and fields of specialization. Some handle only temporary assignments, while others have a temporary service and a permanent personnel agency under the same roof. Some are large national organizations; others are small and strictly local. Some are specialists, focusing on accounting, medical, or legal temporaries; others are generalists which handle primarily office temporaries.

All temporary services, regardless of their size or field of specialization, employ you directly, charge their client companies an hourly rate for your services, and pay you an hourly rate somewhat lower than what the client is paying. Out of this difference, the temporary service must cover Social Security payments, disability payments, liability insurance, fidelity bonding, employer's share of taxes, marketing expenses, advertising expenses, sales expenses, and all office expenses such as rent, payroll expenses, record keeping expenses, cost of submissions to government agencies, the considerable costs entailed in recruiting applicants, and a small profit margin.

Whether you are currently employed, unemployed, looking for your first job, or considering returning to the work force after an absence of some years, temporary work should be considered as a job-search tool; it offers a number of advantages to help put your career plans into motion.

Some Advantages of Temporary Work

Money is an obvious advantage. If you are currently unemployed, temporary work can ease you over the rough spots while you continue to look for a full-time job. Also, you may work as many or as few hours as you wish. Work two or three days a week to cover expenses; spend the rest of the week on your job search.

If you have been away from the work force for some years, you can use temporary employment to help you ease back into the groove without committing yourself to a permanent position. And for a returnee, a beginner, or anyone who is rusty, temporary work can provide a situation whereby you can sharpen up your skills prior to your serious job search.

If you are not sure of your career direction or you would like to have a look inside several different industries before you make a choice, working temporary is the most logical way to go. A month of temporary work can provide intensive, firsthand experience in the fields of your interest—and you get paid to boot!

Working temporary is also an excellent way to get inside and *stay* inside organizations that are ordinarily very hard to crack. Once you are inside an organization as a temporary with an assignment that lasts more than a couple of days, you are a known commodity, not an outsider. If a job opening arises, you'll hear about it first, and you'll have a shot at it before it is announced to the public. It is not uncommon for temporaries to receive job offers when there are no actual job openings at all. A supervisor or personnel officer, upon realizing that a temporary is doing an outstanding job, will often create a new job in the organization in order to convert the temporary to a permanent employee.

In the performing arts—theater, music, dance, and so forth— "temping" is often the way of life between performances. Through temporary work, they are able to keep themselves alive when they are not performing, and they are free to leave the temporary job when a performance beckons.

If you decide to include temporary work in your career plan, be sure to take each temporary assignment as seriously as you would a permanent assignment. By dressing appropriately and conducting yourself in a professional manner, your chances of receiving an excellent permanent job offer will increase dramatically.

NOTE: Temporary work is increasingly reaching out to new fields of employment. Nowadays, there are lawyers and paralegals, nurses

THE HIDDEN JOB MARKET

Lately, there has been a lot of talk about the hidden job market—those jobs which never appear in the want ads and which, obviously, can be filled only by those in the know. Working as a temporary is, in our opinion, one of the best ways to put yourself on the inside of the hidden job market. Furthermore, it provides an arena in which to prove your mettle. It has been estimated that over 50 percent of all job openings are never advertised. Regardless of the accuracy of the estimate, we can say this for a fact—every year, many temporaries are hired as permanent employees by firms for which they had previously been working temporary.

and paramedics, accountants, data and word processors, and other highly trained personnel working temporary. Some of these professionals and paraprofessionals work temporary because they don't want to be tied down to a permanent job; others do it because they want to shop around in the field before deciding on a particular employer. Regardless of your profession, it pays to investigate temporary work before committing yourself to a full-time job.

11

THE SEARCH

Keep Informed

There are those who would argue that the element of chance, or fate, is solely responsible for dealing one person all the lucky breaks, while the next person experiences nothing but misfortune. Over the years, we have had applicants with terrific good luck and those with horrible luck, and we have come to our own conclusion about luck: While chance is surely a factor in all of our lives, you are largely in control of your own fate.

Lucky people always seem to be falling into the right job at the right time, while unlucky people are always missing the boat, either by taking the wrong job or by refusing the right job. Lucky people get hired for positions that don't exist; unlucky people learn that the great sounding job they are trying to get has just been taken off the market. Lucky people hear about jobs that aren't even on the job market; unlucky people miss out on jobs that have been announced for weeks. Lucky people land jobs that they aren't even qualified for; unlucky people spend years learning a skill only to find that there is no longer any need for it.

What we're driving at is that luck, at least the kind of luck we're talking about here, is a function of your *awareness*—awareness of your own strengths and weaknesses, awareness of the local job marketplace, awareness of the changing needs of a given organization or industry, awareness of what's going on below the surface as well as on the surface. Lucky people are like the airplane pilot who always keeps one eye out for an emergency landing strip; they are always on the lookout for an advantageous situation to present itself.

From an unlucky person's point of view, these lucky people never seem to be doing any work; they just have the knack for being in the right place at the right time. Unlucky people spend their time telling stories of the big fish that got away—the job they might have had if only they'd heard about it ten minutes earlier, the promotion they'd have landed if only their supervisor hadn't been fired, the raise they would have got if only the company hadn't announced a new fiscal policy. Unlucky people are much more conscious of luck than are lucky people because most lucky people don't consider themselves lucky. While unlucky people are busy talking about their bad luck, lucky people are out doing their homework.

You see, the luck of the lucky person is usually not luck at all, as much as it is the ability to capitalize on situations that can be of benefit to their careers. This ability doesn't come naturally; it must be developed and nurtured. One of the biggest differences between the lucky and the unlucky is that lucky people keep themselves informed, while unlucky people base their moves on myths, rumors, and half-truths. Lucky people are constantly monitoring the heartbeat of the world around them and are aware of changes as they are happening; they are in the world and of it and are able to *act* accordingly. Unlucky people are always a few beats behind the rest of the world; at best, they *re*act to changing conditions, usually too late to do themselves any good.

The world today is changing at a rate that would have dizzied the job seeker of twenty years ago. Careers that hadn't been invented twenty years ago are today attracting applicants by the thousands; careers that seemed to offer security and high wages twenty years ago are today slipping slowly into obsolescence. Companies take over other companies and are in turn taken over by still larger companies; thousands of jobs are created or destroyed overnight. People quit their jobs without warning, opening their position up to anyone who is qualified and quick enough to get there ahead of the crowd. Somehow, the lucky person always manages to hear the news first.

How can you get lucky? First of all, forget about luck—there's no such thing. Start working on developing the attitude that you are going to know as much about the local, national, and (if necessary) international situation in your field of interest as anyone can possibly know. Decide to break into the local grapevine or start one if one doesn't already exist; it is imperative that you start hearing news from all quarters. Pick up one of the national business magazines or whatever periodicals apply to your fields of interest from time to time, not so much for the specific information they contain as for the overall picture they convey. The financial pages of your daily newspaper probably contain one or two items a week that are of direct interest to you, whether you're an administrative assistant, a steelworker, a banking executive, or just an observer shopping around for a career direction. (It's been said that what you read on the business page today will be on the front page tomorrow.) Finally, for the day-to-day lowdown on your local job marketplace, there's nothing like the want ad section, even if you're not quite ready to start your job search in earnest.

Knowing the lay of the land is important to all stages of your career strategy. In an unscientific survey we recently conducted among a group of Career Blazers' job applicants, we found that at least half of those we spoke with had never read a business magazine or the financial pages of the paper. Why? Most of them said it was "too boring." They couldn't explain how they knew that business news was boring if they'd never even read it; perhaps they were all psychic. What is more likely is that they were all prejudiced against something that— they thought—didn't concern them. When we actually sat down with a few of our applicants and showed them specific articles from the financial pages, the typical reaction was, "Wow, I didn't know that's what they wrote about. I thought it was all numbers and stock market stuff." Here are a few examples of randomly chosen articles that were of interest to our applicants.

● An article about the merger of two companies that make computer chips discussed the future of word processing. This was of great interest to a young applicant who was wondering if she should try to get a job as a secretary immediately or take a word processing course in order to get a better job a few months down the line.

- An article about the problems with the American automobile industry was of great interest to a homemaker about to return to the work force. The article described an environmental organization that was giving the automobile industry a hard time, which got the applicant thinking about a job in a non-profit organization concerned with environmental causes. We eventually found her a job in just such an organization. This was an indirect benefit of reading the financial pages, but an important one nevertheless.

- A young man, just out of college, was shown an article about the fastest growing industries in the state of Washington. He had always wanted to go to the Pacific Northwest but was under the impression that there were no jobs available there. The article convinced him that he ought to give it a try; at least three of the fastest growing fields looked interesting to him.

Keeping informed is not just for executives, politicians, and those who have lots of time on their hands; it is important to *you* to keep tapped into the mainstream. If you have a field of interest, there are publications that specialize in it. If you have no specific field of interest, there are plenty of general interest publications that will keep you abreast of the latest developments in a variety of fields. Set aside a little time every week for reading. You may not see the immediate benefit, but the long-term benefit, especially if it becomes a habit, is unquestionable. Keeping informed, you'll see, will make you lucky— even though we all know there's no such thing!

Keep Records

Keeping a clear record of every résumé you send out, every phone call you make to a prospective employer, every visit to an agency, and—later on—every interview, will make your life a lot easier.

The simplest way to keep a record of your résumés is to make a carbon or photocopy of each covering letter that you used in your mail campaign. On the bottom of the copy, you can note the dates and contents of any phone calls to that employer, plus the date and time of an interview if you set one up. However, don't trust these notes to be your calendar; buy a calendar specifically for this purpose, note dates and times clearly, and *refer to it* every day.

On pages 134–136, we have provided a record-keeping form that allows you to keep track of all the organizations you have contacted— regardless of whether it was through a mail campaign, a personal contact, or an agency—and to follow the progress of your relationships with these organizations through to their conclusions. If you think you'll need more of these pages, photocopy them *before* you fill them out.

Choose
Your Advisors

The problem with letting go of your preconceptions is that, at first, there is nothing to take their place. This can leave a rather frightening gap in your conception of reality, and striving to fill the vacuum as quickly as possible, you may find yourself seeking advice from friends, relatives, neighbors, the mailman, or whomever else happens to be nearby.

Our recommendation is to tread carefully when seeking advisors. It's not that we are opposed to the idea of someone advising you about your career; on the contrary, we feel it is of utmost importance that you have a small number of people who know you well, and who have some knowledge of the local employment situation, to help you plot your course. Problems can arise, though, when you have *too many advisors* or the *wrong kind of advisors*.

It is not uncommon to find a group of experts in a given subject

JOB-HUNTING RECORDS

COMPANY:_____

ADDRESS:_____

NAME OF CONTACT:_____

TITLE:_____

FOUND THROUGH: Agency ( ) name of agency_____

                             Name of counselor_____

                             Phone Number_____

                             Want Ad ( )   Personal Contact ( )

                             Other_____

_____

Sent Résumé ( ) date_____   Phoned ( ) date_____

Interview scheduled for_____
                        (date)   (time)

INTERVIEW: Date_____   Interviewer_____

              Results:_____

_____

Thank you/follow-up letter sent:_____

_____

JOB OFFER? Yes ( )   No ( )

_____

NOTES:_____

_____

JOB-HUNTING RECORDS

COMPANY:_____

ADDRESS:_____

NAME OF CONTACT:_____

TITLE:_____

FOUND THROUGH: Agency (   ) name of agency_____

Name of counselor_____

Phone Number_____

Want Ad (   )   Personal Contact (   )

Other_____

_____

Sent Résumé (   ) date_____   Phoned (   ) date_____

Interview scheduled for_____
                          (date)   (time)

INTERVIEW: Date_____   Interviewer_____

Results:_____

_____

Thank you/follow-up letter sent:_____

_____

JOB OFFER? Yes (   )   No (   )

_____

NOTES:_____

_____

JOB-HUNTING RECORDS

COMPANY:_____

ADDRESS:_____

NAME OF CONTACT:_____

TITLE:_____

FOUND THROUGH: Agency (   ) name of agency_____

Name of counselor_____

Phone Number_____

Want Ad (   )   Personal Contact (   )

Other_____

_____

Sent Résumé (   ) date_____   Phoned (   ) date_____

Interview scheduled for_____
                    (date)   (time)

INTERVIEW: Date_____   Interviewer_____

Results:_____

_____

Thank you/follow-up letter sent:_____

_____

JOB OFFER? Yes (   )   No (   )

_____

NOTES:_____

_____

who cannot come to an agreement on anything that falls within the realm of their expertise. For someone in need of advice, the help of one or two (or perhaps even three) experts can be of enormous benefit. The problems begin when you start talking with too many advisors. Contradictions begin to turn up, one person's opinion seems to cancel out the next person's, and before you know it, you're even more confused than you were before you got advised.

Your advisor's job is to help you formulate your own point of view. "Trying on" an advisor's point of view helps you understand what it's like to have a point of view on that subject. Trying on another advisor's point of view gives you some "triangulation," something against which to measure the first viewpoint. After discussing your predicament with several people—it might mean speaking with as many as ten or fifteen people at first—you should choose the two or three who will be your "cabinet" and stop looking for more advisors. You may, ultimately, come to disagree with some of your advisors' opinions; this is a natural part of coming to your own point of view, and a good advisor will never hold it against you. However, if you don't make your cabinet choices early on, you'll find yourself drowning in a sea of opinions.

Who are the wrong advisors for you? There are three categories of inappropriate choices.

1. Those who know less than you do

2. Those who have a vested interest in seeing that you make a certain decision

3. Those whose expertise does not correspond to your needs

Those who know less than you do might include your kid brother, your next-door neighbor, or the nice man at the dry cleaning shop. Sure, they know you and would go out of their way to help, but what do you know that you don't about preparing *your* career strategy? People love to give advice. Get into the habit of politely tuning out useless advice or at least tuning it down to a low murmur in the background.

Those with vested interests might have the best intentions, such as Scott Lehman's parents, who pressured Scott into becoming a lawyer, or they might have base intentions, such as an unscrupulous employer trying to pressure a naïve job seeker into taking an underpaid position. In any event, look out. A good advisor has no axe to grind, has nothing to gain or lose by the final outcome of your job search, and is committed to encouraging you to develop your own point of view.

Those whose expertise does not quite correspond to your needs are the trickiest ones to discover, especially if you are new to the game. The tendency is to be bowled over by the advice offered by one in a high position. For example, you mention to a friend that you've been offered a position with an engineering firm. Your friend says that her uncle is the president of an engineering supply company that is taking in over $50 million a year in Saudi Arabia alone and that if you like, she'll arrange for you to have a chat with him. You go in and see the old boy who, between cigars, informs you that a smart person would be a fool to take such a low-paying job, that the company in question is notorious for underpaying its top engineers, and that it would be worth your while to keep shopping around. It all sounds convincing when it comes from such an authority, but don't turn down the job, not just yet. Think about a few things first. How much does the old guy make a year, personally? A half-million? A million? Whatever it is, it's a lot, and any salary in your bracket might appear low to him. He said something about the company underpaying top engineers, and you let it slide, but you know that you've only been at it for a couple of years—it'll be a while before you would call yourself a top engineer. Forgetting what he said about the pay, he didn't even know what kind of job you had applied for. Upon close analysis, it appears that this particular captain of industry—however much he might know about his own business—was not necessarily the right advisor for you. He had a clear perspective, strong opinions, immense knowledge, but he just had no idea how *you* fit into the picture. Better find someone else.

Once you've chosen your advisors, stick with them. The only time to dump an advisor is when you discover that he or she somehow slipped into one of the abovementioned categories; the only time to add an advisor to your cabinet is when you meet someone whose knowledge and impartiality far surpass those of your current advisors. Don't change advisors haphazardly!

How do you go about finding good advisors? Unless you need highly specialized information, your best advisors can usually be culled from among people you already know. A friend or relative who works in a field similar to one you are investigating, a current or former guidance counselor, a former employer, the employer of a friend or relative—you'll find that most of these people will be happy to speak with you. It won't take you long to find two or three whose advice will be meaningful for you; and even if none of your original prospects have the necessary qualifications to be a good advisor, surely they'll each know one or two others you can speak with. (Later on, when we discuss the job interview, we'll show you how even an unsuccessful interview can yield a gold mine—in contacts and advisors.)

What if you need more specialized information or if those nearby are not qualified to offer advice? There is an entire industry specializing in supplying people with employment and career advice. The personnel industry comprises résumé writing services, career counseling services, psychological testing services, executive placement services, outplacement services, and permanent and temporary personnel services. Obviously, there is no lack of information or people who are capable of giving you—or selling you—the advice you need.

For the time being, however, you are well advised to stick to your own circle of friends, relatives, and people you meet during the course of your job search. The various elements of the personnel industry will be fully discussed later on in this book; with a little luck, you'll have all the advice you'll need by then.

Keep the Faith

You've already done a lot of work in finding yourself a new job or a new career; it doesn't make sense to waste that effort in a halfhearted job search.

By now you should have a pretty good sense of career direction or at least a narrower set of choices than you had when you were first starting out. You ought to have a good résumé or at least a full set of notes toward a good résumé; you should have your packaging in order; you should have begun talking to your preliminary contacts. The question now is, How do you see yourself? Do you accept yourself as a serious job searcher, as a responsible worker, as someone *you* would hire if you were in charge?

Before you go out and start putting yourself on the line, it is important that you feel comfortable with yourself. This is especially true if you are making a major career and/or life change. If you feel that all this preparation is nothing more than a disguise, a new suit of clothes over the same old you, then you'd better spend the next week or two weeks, or however long it takes, to grow into the you that you'll be presenting to the world.

A good way to do this is to start contacting nonthreatening leads: friends, relatives, old bosses or teachers—people you know and trust. But don't present yourself in the old comfortable way. Come on strong, like the serious job seeker you are. Don't be afraid to hear them say, "You've changed." Pump them for advice, for leads, for information. You won't be nervous about it because you already know these people and because *this is a trial run, not the actual search.* Of course, if you get some information or leads from them, so much the better.

If you find that after a few days of this, you're ready to hit the big time, great! It's time to start following up on want ads, making phone calls, sending out résumés, making appointments for interviews, and otherwise launching your full-scale campaign.

If you're not quite ready for an out-and-out campaign, however, and you've run out of personal contacts to practice on, this is a good time to get in touch with one or more personnel organizations. Talking to a counselor at a personnel agency is one step more serious than talking to old Uncle Bill, but it is not as threatening as having your first major interview with a potential employer. Speaking with a counselor about your career plans is a perfect way to tune up for interviews with employers; in addition, it is an ideal way to arrange to *set up* interviews with employers, either right then, the next day, or whenever you feel you are ready.

A Few Job-Search Tips

Be Comfortable with Your Businesslike Attire.

This is especially important for those who have acquired a new wardrobe to suit their new, businesslike attitude. If you don't feel good in your clothes, if it looks like you're just trying them on for size, they are not doing you any good at all. Get accustomed to them: wear them around the house, wear them over the weekend, get used to presenting yourself in a new way.

Dress for Business Even If You Are Unemployed; Wake Up and Get Dressed As Though You Were Going to Work.

Remember, it *is* work to find a job. Dress for business when you go to speak with an employment agency, when you have an appointment with a personal contact, and even when you are speaking to a friend about your job search. They'll take you more seriously and you'll take yourself more seriously. It may seem silly, but it works.

Dress for Business Even If You Are Sitting at Home Reading the Want Ads or Making Follow-up Phone Calls.

You'd be surprised at the effect it can have on your telephone voice and attitude. In fact, in a recent university experiment, a group of students and teachers was recruited to take telephone calls from a group of approximately forty callers. The callers were a diverse group: young, old, fat, skinny, and from various socioeconomic and ethnic groups. The idea was to see how close the people who answered the calls could come to providing exact descriptions of the callers by knowing only what they sounded like over the telephone. Amazingly enough, the people who answered the phones were almost 100 percent accurate in their descriptions of the callers. They even guessed the weight of their callers to within an average of three pounds, plus or minus! The moral is, you can't hide behind the telephone. Be as serious and businesslike about your phone calls as you are about your personal visits; it will pay off.

As the Boy Scouts Say, Be Prepared.

Have your coffee before you go out for your interviews or before you pick up the phone for your first want ad follow-up call. Assume that you are going to get a job offer *today*. Be "up" for your contacts; your enthusiasm is contagious, and the person across the desk or on the other end of the phone is liable to get enthusiastic and make you a job offer when you least expect it. So expect it.

Unless you are trying to find a job for which you are absolutely unqualified (and by now you should know better), you are probably as likely a candidate as any of the others seeking the same or similar positions. All you need now is faith in yourself, faith to present a positive attitude to your personal contacts and prospective employers. After all, you've done your homework, you know what you're looking for, and you know how to present yourself—you already have a huge jump on the competition.

12

JOB SOURCES

Follow
That Lead!

While it is not impossible to find the job you want on your first try, most job searches require a certain amount of investigative trial and error before they hit pay dirt. Among your most crucial tools in the job search are the personal contacts you start out with and the ones you meet along the way.

After you have obtained your new position, it is easy to look back and see which of your leads panned out and which ones didn't. All but one or two of your leads, in fact, may appear in retrospect to have been useless; that is, all except the ones which actually led you to your new position. This, however, is an illusion; *all* your leads are important for two good reasons.

First, during your search, it is usually impossible to determine which of your leads will pan out and which ones won't. It is often the least likely leads that get you where you want to go, while the ones that seemed most promising are dead ends. So don't judge or edit your leads during the search; follow them all through, and leave the second-guessing until after you've secured your new job.

Second, leads are important as *leads* while you're looking for a job;

they're even more important, potentially, as *contacts* after you've found a job. We're not just talking about the person or persons who helped you find the job; we're talking about *everyone* you dealt with during your search. These are people who have met or spoken with you, who have some sense of who you are, and who have already made a commitment to helping you. Don't forget about them just because you've found a job. Let them know what you're doing. Keep in touch. Perhaps they work in a related field; if they are willing to help you find a job, don't you think they'd be happy to do business with you after you've found a job?

The successful job searcher recognizes the importance of personal contacts. During the search, your leads not only increase your chances of connecting with an interesting job, they help fill you in on local employment conditions in the fields of your interest. Most of the people you speak with, incidentally, will not be offended or annoyed that you are troubling them; on the contrary, they'll be glad to help out, if only by recommending someone else who knows more about the field than they do.

Read the Want Ads

In the ideal job search, you would tell everyone you knew that you were looking for a job in a given field, and they would all go out and speak with everyone they knew in that field, and a few days later you'd start receiving phone calls from employers eager to meet you. However, since this is not an ideal world, both job seekers and employers have to settle for a somewhat less personal, though highly effective, way of making contact with each other—the help-wanted ads.

Help-wanted ads appear in every major newspaper and trade journal and most minor ones as well. Many larger organizations, in addition to advertising locally, will place ads for important positions in the

Sunday New York *Times* help-wanted section for national coverage. Trade magazines and newspapers are a very important advertising medium as well; if you have an interest in a specific field, it is well worth your while to spend a little research time at your library or newsstand looking for the special interest publications that cover that field.

You will find ads both for organizations seeking help and personnel agencies representing such organizations in the help-wanted sections. Agencies, generally, are required by law to state somewhere in the body of their ads that they are, in fact, agencies and not companies advertising directly. Although companies usually identify themselves in their advertising, it is not uncommon for them to place "blind" ads with no corporate identification, using a newspaper or post office box number rather than an identifiable address and phone number.

Personnel agencies generally advertise their best available jobs, their goal being to attract the greatest number of good applicants to come in and register with their agency. Whether or not you get a shot at a particular advertised job depends upon how many other qualified applicants are interested in that job, how soon after the ad runs you appear at the agency, and so forth. Any good agency, however, will have many more jobs available than advertised, many of which are similar to the one you responded to. Often, an agency will run an ad for a job that represents an entire category of jobs that they are trying to fill; by pulling in applicants for that one job, they are really recruiting for the whole category. This increases your chances of being sent out to interview for a job similar to the one you responded to. As new job orders come in every day, even if you miss out on a specific advertised job, there is a good possibility that the agency will soon have another job for you similar to the one advertised.

Companies seeking help directly, on the other hand, usually advertise for a specific position with the intention of pulling in not a large number of applicants but a small number of *highly qualified* applicants. Unlike agencies, which are usually interested in having applicants come in and register, individual organizations are generally interested in seeing résumés first, then calling to arrange a personal meeting if they are interested in your résumé.

Want Ad Tips

Don't Be Put Off by the Job Titles Given in Want Ads.

Don't be afraid of particular job titles. Job titles are the language of want ads, the language of employment. They are not meant to be descriptive or prescriptive, but rather to express telegraphically the general nature of the position in question. Realize that, oftentimes, the person who actually writes the ad knows next to nothing about the position and must guess or approximate in order to have something to say about it. While one ad writer might describe a job as a "gal/guy Friday" position, another might call it an "administrative assistant," while still another might call it "secretary." Same job, same pay, same company, same office, same desk, same everything—different ad. Learn to read between the lines, to see through the job titles to the jobs themselves.

Read All the Ads.

In the same way that there is no way to know for sure how a job is going to be described in the want ads, there is no way to know in advance *where* it is going to be classified. A job in chemical engineering may be listed under "chemical," under "engineers," or under some category that you would never imagine. Someone looking for a position as controller of a large corporation might not want to read the "accountants" section on the theory that those jobs would be below his or her level, but it would be a big mistake; the best controller positions might just as well be listed under "accountants" as anywhere else. Remember that, in addition to the sometimes strange notions of those who write and place want ads, you are up against a whole other problem: the typographical error. By reading the entire section, you might just find the perfect position for a controller listed under "beauticians" or "chemical engineers"!

Be Skeptical of the Qualifications Listed.

Don't be put off by a list of qualifications that you don't have unless you know that they are absolutely essential to the job (which is especially valid in professional and technical occupations). *Very few* jobs are filled by people who precisely meet the advertised qualifications. Many want ads give the *ideal* qualifications, as imagined by a wishful supervisor or personnel officer. Often, the feeling is that by giving tough qualifications, the number of applicants—and thus the amount of screening work—will be kept to a minimum. If you are interested in an advertised position because you're interested in that organization, job title, or field, you should respond to the ad even though your qualifications are not as impressive as those specified in the ad. By going in strong, you stand a good chance of convincing them that you are the right person for the job; we've seen many cases where the personnel officer admitted that the qualifications in the ad really had very little to do with the job itself. And by keeping the number of applicants to a minimum, the ad is doing you a favor by decreasing the competition you'll have to face.

Don't Be Frightened Off by the Requirements.

A similar situation exists here but with a difference. You'll sometimes see qualifications or requirements listed in the want ads that frighten you away not because you don't meet the qualifications but because you *do*—and you don't want to have anything to do with them. The prime example of this is *typing*. A quick glance through the want ads will be enough to prove to you that "good typing," or "type 60 wpm," or any variation on the theme is one of the more popular requirements in the want ad section. The only problem is that many people who know how to type—and type well—simply don't want to type. Therefore, they ignore any ad that mentions typing. We feel that this is a big mistake; many of the jobs that specify typing don't actually entail that much typing. The same is true with stenography; it is often used as a qualification for a job, though you may never have to use it once you are actually employed. However, the people who write the want ads know that there is some light typing involved and figure that as long as there's some typing, they might as well get someone who can do it well. Also, like many other advertised qualifications, it is put there to scare away those who are lazy and unmotivated: "If they think they're too good to type, let them look for a job elsewhere." Don't fall for it; if you're interested in the job, *go for it*.

Be Aware of Promotability.

Two jobs that start out the same way won't necessarily end up the same way. For example, two women obtain administrative assistant positions at the same time. Their starting salaries are the same, their benefits are the same, they both work in nice offices and have wonderful bosses. The only difference is that one is working in a law office while the other is working at a magazine. Regardless of how well she does her job, the one who works in the law office will never become a lawyer unless she starts going to law school at night. But she'll never be *promoted* to that position; it's impossible! The one at the magazine, however, may very well be promoted to an editorial, advertising, or administrative position; it's a common phenomenon. If you are looking for a secretarial, administrative assistant, or other entry-level job, be aware that promotability is more a function of the industry or type of organization than of the job itself. In any of the communications industries such as radio, television, motion pictures, publishing, and advertising; in the nonprofit sector; and in any industry with a highly developed nontechnical end such as fashion, cosmetics, personnel, finance, insurance, real estate, wholesale and retail trade, etc., it is entirely possible to move up the ladder from entry-level. In technical and professional fields, your growth potential is limited if you are not a member of the profession. This by no means indicates a condemnation of employment in these fields; on the contrary, some of the finest administrative positions are available in these fields. For example, a woman we placed as a legal secretary five years ago is today the office manager of her law firm at a salary in the vicinity of $50,000 a year! All it means is that if your goal is to get to the top of a given field and you are starting with an entry-level position, you had better choose a job with a nontechnical or nonprofessional organization.

Be Wary of Ads That List a Salary Much Higher Than Those Listed for Similar Positions.

If the average salary for secretaries is $18,000 and you find one that lists similar qualifications but is paying $30,000, you can bet there's something fishy going on. Companies will sometimes use this ploy to bring in a large number of applicants, tell them that the high-paying job has already been filled, and offer them jobs at normal salaries. It's illegal, but it sometimes happens. Occasionally, a phony ad is used to get information from applicants. For example, a company considering opening a word processing department recently ran an ad for word processors at a somewhat higher than normal salary. Of course, many word processors applied. The company interviewed each one of them, taking names, addresses, current place of employment, and what kind of salary they'd need to consider changing jobs. The data were then analyzed, and the company executives were able to come to a decision based on actual employment/marketplace conditions. In addition, if they decided to go ahead with their department, they had a huge list of word processors to choose from. Needless to say, this sort of practice is unscrupulous—verging on illegal—and certainly a waste of time for those who applied for the job in good faith. The moral: if you spot an ad that looks phony, be wary. Of course, if you think there's a chance it's for real and if it's something you are interested in, then investigate it. Just keep your eyes open.

Above all, you must keep in mind that the job descriptions given in want ads are nothing more than rough approximations of the general parameters of the position. This means that job descriptions often don't have that much to do with the jobs described. Once you have been hired, *you make the job—it doesn't make you.* Jobs grow, shrink, expand, contract, change seasonally and yearly. It is not uncommon for a new job title to be created for a person who has expanded the boundaries of the original job description. It's not inconceivable that you will soon be in the position of *writing* a help-wanted ad—to find someone to replace you in the position that you have outgrown.

Visit Employment Agencies

Why go to an employment agency when you can go straight to the organizations that are looking for help? There is certainly no reason *not* to go directly to the organizations that need help. If you see a corporate help-wanted ad for a position that appeals to you, if one of your personal contacts recommends you to an organization that might have an opening for someone with your talents, or if you have a hot line to the hidden job market either because you are working as a temporary in a company that has an opening or through some other connection, then by all means *go for it*. However, you should be aware that many organizations do not like to do their own recruiting; they don't have the staff or the facilities for it. It is for this reason that they deal with agencies. The agencies have all the "headaches": recruiting and advertising expenses, testing and screening applicants, maintaining a large staff and plenty of space to accommodate hundreds of applicants at a time, and so forth. In exchange for taking on these headaches, the agencies get job orders from their corporate clients. When you visit or send your résumé to a company, you have a shot at one or perhaps a few jobs. When you visit an agency, you have a chance to interview for *many* jobs. That's a pretty good reason for visiting an employment agency.

In the bad old days, agencies often made their job applicants pay for placement out of their own pockets. The usual arrangement was one or two months' salary, payable over an agreed-upon period of time (for example, the first year of employment). Some agencies even made applicants pay *before* they were placed in a job! Nowadays, this latter practice is totally unacceptable, and the former practice is obsolete in all but a few very specific situations. Today, almost all personnel agencies work on a feepaid basis, whereby the company that hires the applicant pays the fee in full. In other words, it costs you *nothing*. The only times you will encounter non-feepaid situations are

1. In certain glamour industries, where there are so many applicants for every job that the organizations refuse to pay the fee and the applicants still keep coming! The theory is that if you want one of these rare jobs badly enough, you'll be willing to pay the fee.

2. In executive counseling situations, where an executive will pay a counseling organization $2,000 or more for a résumé, a covering letter, and assistance in planning a campaign to distribute them.

3. There are still a few places left where the movement to feepaid agencies has not caught on. Fortunately, however,

these places are few and far between; we feel strongly that applicants should never have to pay for placement.

You could look in the Yellow Pages to find a good agency, but that won't really tell you very much. A better bet is to study your newspaper want ad section, concentrating on the agency advertising. You'll find that each agency's ads have a slightly different feel. Some agencies will consistently list jobs that look interesting to you, while others will concentrate on fields that you have no interest in. The best thing to do is to pick out the top two or three agencies and visit them in person. Once in the office, you'll have a chance to judge the agency at close hand. Is the office pleasant or grubby? Are the people helpful and friendly, or are they trying to hustle you into something you don't want? Do they really have the jobs they advertised, or were their ads just a come-on? It won't take long to find the answers to your questions; don't make any commitments until you feel good about the agency.

When you visit an agency, you'll be asked to fill out an application and take whatever skill tests (typing, shorthand, etc.) might be necessary for the type of employment you are seeking. You will have an interview with a counselor, who will explore various career alternatives with you in addition to assessing your packaging and ability to give a good interview. The counselor will advise you as to how realistic he or she thinks your expectations are and will give you an estimate as to how soon you'll be hearing about interview arrangements. It's not unusual for you to be sent out on a number of interviews directly from the agency; so be prepared.

Agencies can—and will—ask a lot of questions about your ability to perform your job. In fact, the better the agency is, the more questions they'll ask; it's their job to know you well. However, there are certain questions which—by law—may not be asked of you. Questions about your age, your color, and your sex are considered discriminatory and therefore illegal. You may not be asked if you have an arrest record. Questions about your national origin are out. If you feel that an agency is asking discriminatory questions, tell them so. If they persist, switch to another agency!

Some personnel agencies are associated with temporary personnel services and may recommend that you try working temporary for a while.

There are some excellent reasons for taking a temporary job, as we have said, but if you are dead set on finding a permanent job, then there's no reason why you should be talked into being a temporary. We do suggest, however, that you hear your counselor out; depending on current market conditions in your field, there may be excellent reasons why no permanent jobs are available at the moment, especially if the industry is seasonal. It might be wise to take a temporary job now with the proviso that as soon as good permanent positions become available, you'll be the first to know.

How do you get an employment agency to work harder for you than for other applicants? This is a selfish—though not at all unreasonable—question. Theoretically, a good agency will work equally hard for all of its applicants. However, agencies are not nonprofit companies; they make their living by *placing* people. Therefore, they tend to work harder for highly placeable applicants than for those who appear to be tough to place. If you've done your homework, however, this should work to your benefit; everything you've done to impress a potential employer—from résumé, to clothes, to your attitude—will be equally impressive to your agency counselor. By all means, take your agency visits seriously; the more serious you are, the more *placeable* you appear to be and the harder the agency will work for you.

What if you don't know what you want? This is a tough one. The problem is, in the words of many a counselor, "If you don't know what you want, how the heck am I supposed to know?" The more certain you are with your counselor, the better your results will be. If this means cheating a little, so be it; choose something arbitrarily and say it in a strong voice. Better yet, *do your homework;* study the employment situation and have a pretty good sense of direction *before* you talk to a personnel counselor. Counselors usually know their business, but they're not mind readers.

Sometimes it happens that an agency can't find you a job right away. And, unless the agency you choose is so small that you're the only applicant they've seen all week, there are plenty of other applicants who may be slightly more placeable than you are. But you shouldn't let this get you down; you *are* highly placeable, and you're going to get a good job one way or another. *Call your counselor every day* to see if anything new has developed. Don't worry about being a pest; in the job market, it's considered a positive attribute! Make sure your counselor knows who you are and what you want. If a week goes by and you feel you're being given the brush-off, it may be time to try a new agency.

Outplacement and Executive Search

You've probably heard of outplacement and executive search organizations without quite knowing what they were. Here, to set the record straight, are our pocket synopses.

Outplacement services help companies find new jobs for their employees. This is often needed when a company is moving to a new location and can't take its employees along, when a company is going out of business entirely, leaving its employees with no visible means of support, or when an executive is being let go.

Executive search is that branch of the personnel industry dealing exclusively with high-level executive placement. Corporations come to executive search firms when filling gaps in upper-echelon management; individual executives generally do *not* apply to executive search firms for a position.

Summary

It would be disingenuous for us to pretend to be impartial about the personnel business—we are in the business, we've been in it for over thirty years, and we think it's a great business. We don't claim that the only way—or even the best way—for you to find a new position is to seek the help of a personnel agency; the only best way is the way that works best for you. However, if you have no better place to begin or if your other contacts have failed to pan out, then you can't go wrong by paying a visit to your local employment professionals. It's their job to know the marketplace inside and out, to know which employers can best utilize your talents, to know which positions can take you where you want to go.

What is, perhaps, most important to remember when you're considering whether or not to make contact with a personnel service is this:

You and your personnel agency share a common goal: getting you a job.

Personnel agencies don't get paid until you get hired. You can bet that they'll do whatever they can to place you in just the sort of position you're looking for.

THE INTERVIEW

All the work you've done so far has been leading up to one event: the interview. Regardless of how you got in touch with an organization—through a personal contact, an agency, or temporary work—the interview is an integral step in the hiring process. No one is hired "sight unseen."

To many people, interviews are the most frightening part of the job hunt. One of our applicants, who had been an actress before she decided it was time for a career change, described interviewing as being forced out on a bare stage, in front of a critical audience, without having had a chance to memorize one's lines.

This may be the way most applicants feel about interviews, but it doesn't have to be true for *you*. Let's address our former actress-applicant's fears in order.

- No one is forcing you. You are the one seeking the position, and the interview is a bridge you must cross to get to that position. You should be looking forward to it.

- In general, your audience will not be critical. Interviewers spend their days looking for people to say Yes to; it gives them no joy to say No.

- You already know your lines—it's your life, isn't it?

The real problem is that no job seeker has very much interview experience. Even someone who has had a long career comprising many different jobs cannot have had more than a couple of dozen interviews; most of us have had only a handful of them. When we imagine the "confrontation" with an interviewer who speaks with perhaps eight or ten people every day, it seems an unfair contest.

Interestingly enough, most interviewers would agree that it's unfair, although they would state emphatically that it's not a contest. What's unfair, they would say, is that most job seekers perceive the interview as some sort of confrontation when, in fact, it is a meeting—presumably between equals—to determine if the parties can be of benefit to each other. It's unfortunate, from the interviewers' point of view, that job seekers don't always know this because the sense of confrontation tends to make the interviewee nervous, causing a bad interview and the inevitable rejection of someone who may have been perfectly suited to the position. And interviewers are not paid to reject applicants; their job is to find those applicants capable of making a contribution to their organization.

Make the Most of the Interview

The interview is the place where you make your résumé "come to life" in the form of—you! It is the forum whereby you can maximize your good points, minimize your bad points, and stress your personality factors. In addition, it is the place where you have an opportunity to find out about the organization, to get the answers to your questions, to see if the position is right for you, to get a sense of what the company is like.

If you had sent in your résumé as part of your direct-mail campaign and you were invited to an interview, remember:

Your résumé has already done most of your selling job. If it hadn't, you wouldn't have been invited to an interview.

In other words, you don't have to worry whether or not the company is interested in you—they are. Even if you were not specifically invited to the interview on the basis of your résumé (if, for example, a personal contact set up the interview without showing anyone your résumé), there is nothing to worry about. As long as you have done your homework, you'll do fine.

One thing you might not anticipate is that the interviewer may start giving *you* a sales pitch about the company. Many an organization has lost an applicant it wanted badly because the interviewer described a less attractive working environment than one of its competitors. So if you suddenly find that you are the recipient of such a pitch, don't be surprised; just sit back, listen closely, and don't be afraid to ask a few good questions.

Your résumé—and verbal résumé—detail the specifics that any potential employer needs to know, but it is the intangibles that so often determine whether or not an applicant is offered a job. The three most important intangibles are

Enthusiasm

We don't mean a bubbling exuberance but rather a straightforward, alert interest in the job, the company, the interview itself. When you've done your homework, incidentally, your interviewer will know it; the sense of enthusiasm will be conveyed. Never act cool or bored! There's nothing that has a more negative effect on an interviewer.

Sincerity

Be yourself. Remember, you've done your homework; in many cases, you've already impressed someone in the organization with

DOING YOUR HOMEWORK

To ensure successful interviews, a little homework is necessary.

Prepare your "verbal" résumé: The résumé you've written down is an outline of your career history. Now is the time to fill in that outline—in your own mind—so that you'll have something to say when your interviewers ask you to tell them about one or another or your résumé entries. The best way to do this is to write a short paragraph about each entry, preferably one that goes into a little detail about your accomplishments in the position. Don't duplicate the information you've put in your résumé, but say something that adds to that information. After you have written your paragraphs, say them aloud several times until you have a good feel for them. If it helps, practice in front of a mirror, or with a friend acting as the interviewer. But remember—don't memorize your lines; you'll sound stiff and stilted if you do.

Do some research on the company: Interviewers are impressed when you show that you know something about the company. Don't just blurt it out, however; slip it into the "warp and woof" of the interview. A well-placed question—about a recent merger, a new product line, a recently appointed vice president—is a a subtle way of demonstrating that you've done your homework.

NOTE: Good questions will produce good answers, which will increase your knowledge of the organization and help you to know which of several companies may be right for you. Bad questions not only will not contribute to your knowledge, they'll also be spotted by your interviewer and are likely to detract from the good impression you're trying to make.

Your verbal résumé preparations need be done only once, although you may need to refresh your memory from time to time if your interviews stretch out over a period of weeks. The company research, obviously, must be individualized to the companies in question. The small amount of time you spend preparing for your interviews will help make you a confident interviewee, and you'll be paid back many times over with positive, successful interviews—and solid job offers.

your credentials—that's why you were invited to the interview. You don't need to pretend you're someone you're not. Assuming a persona that is not your own is sure to make for a disastrous interview; there is no way you'll be able to keep it up over the duration of the interview. Don't try to be the kind of person you think the company is looking for; they may be sick of their type of employee, and that may be why they wanted to speak with you in the first place. If you are nervous, don't try to hide it, especially by acting cool. It's expected that you'll be a little nervous, and the interviewer will make allowances for it and do his or her best to put you at ease. By being yourself, you'll be relaxed; by acting like someone else, you're bound to appear nervous.

Honesty

You don't have to lie about yourself; you've already told the truth about yourself in your résumé—haven't you?—and it's too late to start faking it now. Once you start lying, it's hard to stop. It's also hard to *remember* what you've said, and it's bound to catch up with you. Interviewers are good at spotting discrepancies between what you say and what your résumé says; don't think you'll be able to quickstep your way out of a lie. Needless to say, your lying will increase your nervousness, and you'll lose more by being overly nervous than you'll gain by faking your history. If you are asked a question that you cannot answer, just say, "I don't know." You're not expected to know everything; an honest answer will be appreciated, whereas a dishonest guess will be recognized and held against you.

First impressions are important. Dress properly, which means don't overdress, don't underdress; dress more or less as you would if you had the job. When you enter the interviewer's office, observe where you are. A comment on something in the office—a painting, an unusual paperweight, and so forth—will help establish a cordial, friendly atmosphere right from the start. Don't, however, pick up anything from the desk; don't light a cigarette unless the interviewer offers you one or asks if you'd like to smoke; and, by all means, don't go in chewing gum!

Other Do's and Don'ts

1. **Do** arrive on time. If you are delayed for any reason, phone as soon as you can and reschedule the interview for later that day or early the next.

2. **Do** fill out any application forms in their entirety even if some of the information has already appeared on your résumé.

3. **Do** be well-rested, poised, alert. Watch your posture; don't sprawl in the waiting room or the interviewer's office.

4. **Do** ask questions, if you have any. The idea is not for the interviewer to do all the asking; you are expected to have questions of your own—just make sure they're *good* ones.

5. **Do** be polite. Some interviewers attempt to stir up your antagonism with provocative questions; don't let this ruffle your feathers.

6. **Don't** overbook. One interview per morning, one per afternoon; any more than that is taking chances.

7. **Don't** attempt to steal the floor from the interviewer; don't attempt to interview the interviewer. This runs contrary to a current theory about how to have a successful interview, but we have spoken to many interviewers who are getting sick of applicants attempting to turn the tables on them. Remember, the interviewer practically lives behind that desk; it's pointless for you to try to control the territory. Ask your questions, make your points, but don't dominate—it may make you feel good, but it won't generate any job offers.

8. **Don't** ask a lot of questions about paid holidays, vacations, sick days, personal days, and so on. The last impression you want to create is that you're interested only in how *little* work you'll have to do.

9. **Don't** come in with props such as letters of reference, college report cards, work portfolios, etc., unless you are specifically requested to do so.

10. **Don't** hide behind sunglasses; don't sit on your hands; don't cover your mouth when you speak. These mannerisms indicate that you have something to hide, and every interviewer knows it.

11. **Don't** be vague. Answer questions clearly, definitely. If you don't know an answer, just say so.

12. **Don't** indicate that you have no idea what you want to do. If you're asked what kind of work you'd like to do, saying, "I don't know—anything you've got," does not qualify as a positive answer.

13. **Don't** bring up the subject of salary unless the interviewer says, "Okay, you're hired," without having first discussed salary; in that case, it's your obligation to say, "Great. Now, let's discuss the details." In most cases, the interviewer will bring up the subject; it is generally not discussed in detail until the job offer is made (which we'll talk about in the next chapter).

14. **Don't** knock your current or former employers. It is very likely that you'll be asked for your opinions regarding your employers; keep your answers positive. Negativity will be taken as an indication of what can be expected of you in the future.

15. **Don't** rush your answers, but don't ramble on pointlessly. If it seems that your interviewer is cutting you off in the middle of your answers, perhaps your answers are too long.

It is impossible to predict the exact questions that you'll be asked in your interview; each interviewer has his or her own set of favorites. As long as you have done your homework and as long as you are reasonably relaxed, you shouldn't have any trouble answering whatever is asked of you. The purpose of the interview, from the interviewer's point of view, is, in large measure, *to meet you*—to see how you look and how you speak, to assess how well you'll fit in with the other employees in your prospective department. Some of the questions you'll be asked may seem irrelevant, and some may seem purely social. Go along with it good-naturedly—there's method behind the interviewer's apparent madness.

While it's not a bad idea for you to ask what happened to your predecessor in the position, it is not necessarily a good idea to ask where the job will lead in two or three or five years. As we have said before, you make the job, the job doesn't make you. Once you are on the inside, you'll have ample opportunity to observe the landscape and make decisions about your next career move. By appearing to be too curious about where the job is leading, you're tipping off the interviewer that you don't really understand how things work. It is understood that a person with enthusiasm and initiative determines for him or herself what the next move shall be.

Answering Challenges

Interviewers are experts at zeroing-in on what seem to be the weak points in your résumé. By objecting to these points, they are actually handing you a golden opportunity to prove yourself, to build an airtight case for your suitability. In most cases, the first person who interviews you is not the person who will make the final hiring decision. To ensure that you are passed along to the next level of decision makers, you must make a strong, clear impression on your interviewer. Remember that every time an interviewer okays a prospective new employee for further consideration, he or she must be able to justify that choice. Make it easy for your interviewer by stressing your strong points and fielding objections smoothly. When you do encounter an objection, you should instantly translate it into a question, then answer the question authoritatively. For example:

INTERVIEWER: I notice in your résumé that you don't have an MBA. We were really looking for someone with an MBA, you know.

TRANSLATION: Your résumé looks great, and I like you a lot. I think you can do the job, but you don't have the degree. Can you prove to me that even without the MBA I ought to hire you?

YOUR REPLY: I considered going for an MBA after I graduated from college, but IBM made me an offer that was too good to resist, and I went with it. As you can see, in the four years I was there, I rose very quickly up the ladder. I was responsible for increasing sales by over 250 percent in all three departments I was in charge of, and in my last year, that rose to 300 percent. I think that my experience in the field more than compensates for the lack of the degree.

INTERVIEWER: I see that you were unemployed for almost six months. What was the problem?

TRANSLATION: I love your résumé, but I'm always suspicious of long periods of unemployment, especially when they are recent. Can you allay my fears?

YOUR REPLY: No problem at all. I just felt that I was growing stale after eight years behind the desk, and I felt that as a magazine editor, it wasn't fair to my readers to let myself go stale. So I decided to take some time off and travel around the country. I had enough money saved, so I bought a used camper and headed west. Those articles I wrote recently were written on the trip, incidentally—I took my typewriter with me. After four months, I realized that the best way for me to put my talents to use and to incorporate my love of travel into my work would be to edit a travel magazine—which is why I'm here talking to you.

INTERVIEWER: I see you haven't had a job for, let's see, twenty-two years. That's quite a while to be out of touch with working, isn't it?

TRANSLATION: I'm sure you're qualified to be an administrative assistant with this organization, but can you tell me why?

YOUR REPLY: It is a while. I stopped working when my first daughter was born, and I didn't really consider getting back to it until the youngest was about to go off to college. I'll tell you a little secret, though; raising four kids and managing a household was a lot more demanding than my last secretarial job! And

I know that I'm a lot more capable of dealing with people and handling pressure situations than I ever was back then. I've just finished taking a typing and shorthand refresher course, so my skills are back to where they were. I'm going to make a much better administrative assistant than I would have twenty-two years ago.

What are the weak points in your résumé? Put yourself in an interviewer's place and study your résumé with a critical eye. Pick out your five weakest points, state them as objections, and list them in the spaces below.

1._____

2._____

3._____

4._____

5._____

Now study these objections until you understand how to translate them into questions. Rephrase them as questions below.

1._____

2._____

3._____

4._____

5._____

Remember that the interviewer is not objecting in order to "get" you but simply to see how well you can field objections. Formulate clear, positive answers to the questions; turn apparent weak points into strong points. In the spaces below, write down the key words or phrases of your answers to the objection-questions.

1._____

2._____

3._____

4._____

5._____

Study the objections, the translations, and your answers before each interview—they could come in very handy. If an interview is coming up where you know that a specific new objection will be stated (for example, an interview with an organization that usually requires of its applicants a specific career experience that you lack), make sure you work out your response before going into the interview.

Following Up

Before you leave the interviewer's office, be sure to thank him or her for the time spent with you. If you haven't already discussed it, now is the time to set a date for a follow-up phone call or meeting. If the interviewer has determined that you are absolutely not right for the job, you'll probably be told then and there. If the interviewer feels that you have a shot at the job, a follow-up date will, in all likelihood, be set for the near future.

Why not just come out and tell you that you're hired? Well, in most cases, it's not that simple. Many times, the interviewer does not have final hiring authority. There's no harm, by the way, early in the interview, in asking who does have that authority or in asking about the corporate structure, at least insofar as it relates to your prospective position. There are probably a number of other applicants still to be interviewed; even if the interviewer is convinced that you are the right one, it is customary—and courteous—to give the other candidates a chance to prove themselves. Furthermore, it is better for *you* if you have a few days to think things over, perhaps to do a little more research on the company, to have some more interviews, to reconsider whether you really want to change jobs after all.

Always follow up an interview with a thank you note (see pages 167–170). This not only is common courtesy, it also keeps your name alive with the interviewer; if there is a close contest between you and another candidate, it may tip the balance your way. Even if you have decided to take a position with another company, send a thank you note; there may be a time in the future when the contact will come in handy. If you have received and accepted a job offer, a note of confirmation should be sent to the interviewer and to the person who made the offer (if someone other than the interviewer). Finally it is always a good idea to send a thank you note to a contact who put you in touch with an employment opportunity whether or not that opportunity panned out.

Read the samples of thank-you letters. Obviously, your particular situation—and your ingenuity—will imbue the letters you write with a character all their own. Remember: keep them short, neat, businesslike, and friendly.

FOLLOW-UP THANK YOU NOTE TO AN INTERVIEWER:

May 1, 19—

Ms. Ann Crosby
ABC International, Inc.
456 Pennsylvania Avenue
Youngstown, Ohio 44606

Dear Ms. Crosby:

I just wanted to tell you how pleased I was to meet with you yesterday and how good it feels to know that I am being considered for the position of administrative assistant to Mr. Brock. The job is exactly what I am looking for, and I feel confident that I'll be able to fit right in with the others at ABC International.

Thanks again, and I look forward to hearing from you soon.

Sincerely,

Barbara Kegan

FOLLOW-UP NOTE CONFIRMING REFUSAL OF JOB OFFER:

June 1, 19—

Ms. Ann Crosby
ABC International, Inc.
456 Pennsylvania Avenue
Youngstown, Ohio 44606

Dear Ms. Crosby:

I regret that your job offer came a day too late; just yesterday I accepted a position with another firm. However, I was very pleased to meet you and quite impressed with everything I learned about ABC International.

It was an honor to receive your offer, Ms. Crosby, and, again, I'm sorry that I had to turn it down. Perhaps at some future date, we will have the occasion to work together.

Sincerely,

Barry Stein

FOLLOW-UP NOTE CONFIRMING JOB ACCEPTANCE:

July 1, 19—

Ms. Ann Crosby
ABC International, Inc.
456 Pennsylvania Avenue
Youngstown, Ohio 44606

Dear Ms. Crosby:

I an delighted to confirm my acceptance of the job as
media buyer. I have given my present firm two weeks' notice and will be ready to report to you on July 15.

As you know, I feel that this job is perfect for me
and that I will be able to make a strong contribution to
the continued success of ABC International. I couldn't
be happier!

Sincerely,

Louise Montefuscu

**FOLLOW-UP THANK YOU NOTE TO A CONTACT
WHO REFERRED YOU TO A JOB OPPORTUNITY:**

August 1, 19—

Mr. Raymond P. Hartfield
88 Elm Street
Hingham, Massachusetts 02043

Dear Ray:

  Thank you for letting me know about the media buyer
position at ABC International. I had an interview the
other day with Ann Crosby, and, just this morning, they
made me a job offer which I am planning to accept.

  I can't tell you how happy I am to be getting this position; as you know, I've been moving in this direction
for years, and this was the break I needed. And I'd like
to thank you, Ray, for taking the time to let me know
about it and helping make my dream a reality.

  All the best to Marcia and the kids—let's get together
soon.

Sincerely,

Norm Thalon

14

CHANGING PLACES

When the Job Offer Comes

Job offers sometimes are made toward the close of your first meeting with a representative of an organization, but it is much more common for them to follow at a later date. The offer may come in the form of a telephone call, stating that the job, as discussed, is being offered to you. It may also come during the course of a second interview—this time, perhaps, with someone higher up the corporate ladder than your original interviewer or with the person who will be your supervisor if you choose to accept the position. Your first job offer is the proof that your career strategy is paying off, and you have our permission to breathe a sigh of relief.

This isn't to say that the search is over—unless your first job offer happens to be from the company at the very top of the list, for the job you want, and at the right salary. We suspect, though, that you'll want to be a little cagey when the job offers start coming in. After all, you're not after the first job; you're after the best job. Right?

What do you do when you've received a job offer from a company that you're not sure of, but your other job offers haven't come in yet?

Our advice on this issue is going to be hard-nosed and pragmatic: Accept the job offer with the understanding that you have to give notice at your current job and won't be able to start for two or three weeks. Then, continue pursuing your other job offers. This effectively takes the job off the market and gives you the security of having a bona fide job offer under your belt, which makes you very strong in the interviews and job negotiations to follow. If a better job comes along, you'll just have to tell the first people, "I'm sorry."

It is important at the time a job offer is presented to you that you receive *all* the information pertinent to the job. This means that you can ask all the questions you didn't ask during the interview: How regularly does the company review salaries? Is there a bonus or stock plan? What are the details of the health plan? Is there a dental plan? What about vacations? In addition, you must take into account the location of the company. Will you have to move? Do you want to move? Will your daily transportation expenses minimize the effect of the higher salary a particular company is offering? Is it convenient to cultural centers or shopping centers, for that matter? Will it take you away from the things you like to be near?

As we have stressed before, money is not the only constituent of your income. Now that you have some concrete job offers, you must weigh the various pluses and minuses of each offer, which is trickier than simply going for the one that offers you the most money. The most money may not even be the most money; there are situations where the cost of transportation alone can run to over $1,000 a year. If you are to accurately know how much money you'll be making at a particular job, you must take everything into account.

Look closely at the benefits package. It may not seem very important now, but if you get sick or twist your knee playing basketball, those benefits will suddenly be awfully important. Some companies offer a dental plan, which could be worth hundreds or even thousands of dollars a year to you. Some offer medical plans that include reimbursement, or partial reimbursement, for psychological care. It's a big mistake to ignore the benefits when comparing job offers; it's bad reasoning to assume that you'll never take advantage of them just because you've never yet missed a day of work due to ill health or a twisted knee.

Finally, if given the choice between a high-paying job you think you are going to hate and a low-paying job you think you'll love, or a good-sounding job with a bad company and a mediocre job with a company you'd like to be with, you must be very careful. In general, we recommend that you *take the job you feel good about*. The money may not be as good at first, but remember this: when you feel good about a job, you work harder at it, you learn faster, you progress faster. And that means greater job satisfaction and, ultimately, more money for you. What we have said about working temporary is also true for full-time positions; being on the inside puts you on the hidden job grapevine. A mediocre position with a good company puts you in a prime position to grab the next good job as it opens up. We have a little expression for this:

Proximity is the mother of opportunity.

When a number of job offers are presented to you, take the long-range viewpoint, the *career* viewpoint. It doesn't make sense to do this much work and to come this far only to let a great—though low-paying—career opportunity slip by simply to assuage your immediate pecuniary compulsions.

Negotiating the Salary

The subject of salary will, in all probability, be brought up by your interviewer. In actuality, you will most likely have a pretty good idea about the numbers even before your interview, either from the company's want ads or through your own research. Until you are speaking with the person actually responsible for the hiring decision, it is best to avoid stating specifically the salary you are looking for. If an interviewer asks you to state your salary needs, try to turn it around. Ask how much the company generally pays for the position, then mildly agree that it sounds about right. The theory here is that preliminary interviewers have been known to veto a candidate for salary reasons alone; but if you get past the preliminary interviewer to a real decision maker, you're likely to find that your salary demands will be met if the decision maker wants you for the job. The key is getting in to speak with the decision maker.

NOTE: If asked what your current salary is, don't exaggerate *too* much—they might check up on you. If they do check up, a small exaggeration, even up to a few thousand dollars a year, can be explained away as bonuses and benefits. Any more than that, though, will sound like what it is—baloney!

A company will seldom break off a job offer discussion simply because you are asking for too much money. In all likelihood, they'll bargain with you, perhaps throwing in an extra benefit, a stock plan, or a special bonus instead of an out-and-out salary increase. Obviously, if you really want the job, you'll be willing to come down a little bit in exchange for happiness and future considerations. If you and the company are right for each other, you'll find a way to come to terms.

NOTE: Play hard-to-get; don't discuss your current salary at all unless you know that a job offer is about to be made.

Giving Notice

When accepting a job offer, make it clear to your prospective employer that you won't be able to start for two or three weeks; you have to give your employer notice and wrap up loose ends before leaving. Not only does this give you a chance to evaluate other job offers or seek a counter offer from your current employer, it also underlines your thoughtfulness. If, on the other hand, you say, "I'll start tomorrow, the hell with my boss," your new employer is liable to have second thoughts about you, and it's not too late to cancel the job offer. It is

THE COUNTER OFFER

If you like your current position, but you feel you are underpaid, you don't have to grin and bear it. Start searching for another job as vigorously as if you hated your job. You'll find that your interviews are fun because there's really nothing at stake; you can consider it practice for some future time when you really are desperate for a job. You'll also find that the job offers will start coming in—good job offers.

When you have a few job offers that you are seriously considering, have a meeting with your boss and lay it on the line; unless a suitable counter offer is made, you're going to move on. If your organization likes you as much as you like it, you'll receive an offer that equals or tops the other offers. If not, well, you already have a number of good offers waiting for you.

expected that you won't be starting for two or three weeks—why rock the boat?

There is one exception to this: the boss who won't accept a two weeks' notice. In other words, you give your boss a two weeks' notice, and he tells you to pack your bags and get out immediately or he's calling the sheriff! If you know that this is how your boss operates, and you'd like to start your new job immediately, simply tell your new employer, "I'm going to give two weeks' notice, but Mr. Smith may not accept it. Is it all right, if that's the case, to start the day after tomorrow?" They'll probably be delighted.

On the other hand, if your boss tells you to pack it in immediately, you may not want to say anything to your new employer. After all this work, you could probably use a two-week vacation.

One last note on quitting: when the time finally comes, do it gracefully. It serves no purpose to engage in a serious job search, work hard at your current job, find a great new position, and then storm into your boss's office to tell him how unfair you think he is. Give notice nicely; all you really have to say is that you've found a new position. Period. Although you may not be able to foresee it now, some of your most important contacts in the future may be your previous employers and colleagues; don't alienate them by making a scene when you quit.

On the Job

Your job offers came in; you considered the merits of each position; you politely rejected the ones that didn't appeal to you and negotiated with the ones that interested you; and finally, you reached an amenable agreement with the employer of your choice. Congratulations on your new job!

Now what?

We hope that we've been able to convey the importance of *career* thinking—long-range thinking as opposed to day-to-day, job-to-job thinking. The career thinking that you've applied to your job search must now be applied to your job. Getting the job is only the beginning!

How do you apply career thinking to your job? First and foremost, by doing your job well. Small thinkers don't like to work hard; they think it benefits their employer too much if they do. Big thinkers—career thinkers—work hard because they know that they themselves are the prime beneficiaries of that work. Not only does hard work bring higher pay, promotions, and advances, but also it makes your work more interesting, more fun, and more educational. Let the others think they are getting away with something. While they're busy planning ways to goof off, you'll be sailing ahead on your career journey.

What do you owe your employer? Back in the old days, a worker was expected to stay with an employer for years and years. Nowadays, of course, it's just the opposite; you're looked upon as an odd duck if you stay with the same employer for more than four or five years! No, loyalty to an employer these days is not interpreted as a "marriage till death do you part"; rather, it is—or ought to be—the attitude that as long as you're with this employer, you're going to give it your all. This means putting in a good day's work, using all your ingenuity to help solve company problems, maintaining your enthusiasm, and working well with other staff members.

What do you owe yourself? In the beginning, what you owe yourself and what you owe your employer are synonymous. By doing your job to the best of your ability, you are doing what's best for your career. It is later on that the two paths may begin to diverge.

Somewhere down the line, when you have mastered your job, made your innovations, made your mark on the organization, perhaps received a number of promotions, there may come a time when you find yourself looking around for something else. By then, of course, you'll know a lot more than you know about your field. You'll have plenty of insight into the industry; you'll have a very good sense of direction; and you'll have contacts from whom you can get advice or leads to hidden job openings. Of course, you may not even want to leave the company you're with, and by then you'll know enough about company politics to know exactly what your chances are of getting promoted to a position you really want—and with whom to speak to facilitate that promotion.

Should you decide that it's time to switch companies, you should definitely not allow your conscience to hold you back. You owe it to yourself to start up a new job search right away. This time around, of course, your search will be more sophisticated than the last time; not only do you already know the principles involved, you also have contacts, information, and a certain reputation in your field. With any luck, your future job searches will be a breeze compared with this one.

In fact, for many knowledgeable people, the job search is an ongoing constant of life. They are always sensitive to industry trends, to innovations in the field, and to the hirings and firings that create job openings in their own and other organizations. Once you've been on the inside for a little while, the industry perspective will snap into view. You'll suddenly have a very good sense of which companies are on the way up, which are on the way down, which ones are good to work for, and which ones drive their employees crazy. You'll be able to use this information to help determine what your next move ought to be.

In fact, once you have successfully placed yourself in the field of your choice, you may never again have to search for a new position. You'll find—if you've been doing a good job—that the offers will seek you out. At parties, industry functions, or even at the supermarket, you're liable to run into a colleague from another organization who says, "By the way, let's get together for lunch next week. We have a little proposition you might be interested in."

The key is to be on the *inside* of the field of your choice. Few satisfactions in life can compare with the satisfaction that accompanies a job well done; few people are happier than those whose lives revolve around a satisfying career. We hope that this book has contributed to your understanding of how to choose . . . change . . . and advance *your* career so that you can experience that satisfaction for yourself.

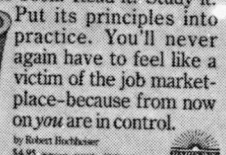

Getting Your Words Across
Murray Bromberg and Milton Katz
224 pp., $3.95
A unique new basic vocabulary book utilizing brief articles, exercises and crossword puzzles to help build word power.

A Pocket Guide to Correct Punctuation
Robert Brittain   96 pp., $1.95
Explains what each mark means, and shows how to use it with clarity and precision.

A Pocket Guide to Correct English
Michael Temple   128 pp., $1.95
A concise guide to the essentials of correct grammar and usage, spelling, punctuation, writing, and more.

A Pocket Guide to Correct Spelling
Francis Griffith   256 pp., $1.95
A handy quick-reference tool that lists 25,000 words in alphabetical order, correctly spelled and divided into syllables.

Barron's "Easy Way" Series: English Titles
Three practical guides filled with straightforward instruction and numerous examples. Ideal for students or anyone else who needs the practice.

English the Easy Way
Harriet Diamond and Phyllis Dutwin
224 pp., $5.95

Spelling the Easy Way
Joseph Mersand and Francis Griffith
144 pp., $5.95

Typing the Easy Way
Warren T. Schimmel and Stanley A. Lieberman
144 pp., $6.95

Encyclopedia of English Terms
Benjamin Griffith   320 pp., $6.95
Defines hundreds of essential terms, with in-depth explanations and many helpful examples. All areas are covered: grammar and usage, literature, composition.